THE LONDON APPRENTICE

THE
LONDON
APPRENTICE

by GIL JACKSON

PUBLISHED IN THE UNITED KINGDOM

Copyright © Gil Jackson, 2016
All rights reserved.

First edition: 2016
Second edition 2020

The London Apprentice
Typeset 12/16 pt Perpetua

Paperback ISBN: 978-1-8382326-5-8
EBook ISBN: 978-1-8382326-4-1

No part of this publication may be reproduced, stored in a retrieval system or transmitted in any form or by any means, electronic, mechanical, photocopying, recording, or otherwise, without the prior permission of the author and the publisher of this book.

Author's address: **gilvjackson@hotmail.co.uk**

Cover artwork, EPaper make-up and formatting by:
www.hirambgood.co.uk

EBook version formatting to industry standards by:
www.hirambgood.co.uk

HTML and CSS Validated.

DEDICATED

To mum and dad,
Ida Eileen Stevens, 1910−96;
Ernest Reginald Jackson, 1908−95

As well as all those compositors that made the printed word what it is today

OTHER WORK

FICTION:
The Seventh Gift
The Tinners Hut

NON-FICTION:
Hiram B. Good's
Multi-Drop Training Bible
Hiram B. Good's
From Stone to Amazon

CONTENTS

Prologue	8
1 – The Line is On	15
2 – The Composer	25
3 – The Reading Room	38
4 – Distributing	42
5 – Cleaners and Tea-Breaks	50
6 – The Binding Ceremony	58
7 – Print School	67
8 – Trots and Trotting	78
9 – Tickets Please!	88
10 – Soho	92
11 – A Wet Lunch	98
12 – Big Red	110
13 – Transport and Accidents Waiting to Happen	115
14 – The Beano	124
15 – Swearing and Other Terms of Endearment	131
16 – Twenty-Four Hours from Tulsa	133
17 – A Suspected Criminal for a Day	136
18 – An Oasis in London	143
19 – Mumping: An Augment to Wages	150
20 – The Cat	156
21 – Times Up	162
22 – The Line is Cut	169
23 – The End of the Line	179
24 – Printing Trade Terms	181
Bibliography/Acknowledgments	187
Biography	188
About the Author	189
Other Books by the Author	190

PROLOGUE

A WORD about this biography of mine. Everything written happened. Not necessarily word for word, but as near as any author can be when trying to recall the past. As Eric Morecambe replied to Andre Previn after his criticism of his playing of Grieg's Piano Concerto in the 1971 Morecambe and Wise Show: 'I'm playing all the right notes; not necessarily in the right order.'

I came out of my apprenticeship in 1967 and began writing *The London Apprentice* four years later; so, the recall of past events was comparatively fresh. The main frame of the book was written pen on paper before being transferred to a typescript where it sat until the printing industry began to change from what was known as hot-metal into phototypesetting computers. From there, I managed to copy my manuscript onto a paper ASCII tape that drove a Linotron CORA 5 digital phototypesetting system. The intention being that one day it would save a publisher having to re-set it. From here the paper tape moved to a seven-inch floppy disk where it was again downloaded. Then along came another company and a different process – the ITEK System. While working as the origination manager with a Plymouth based magazine and book-setting company I managed to find a boffin at ITEK's West London head office who reckoned he could transfer Linotron's CORA 5 onto the ITEK System of coding. I sent the tape to him at their London office along with other tapes that the company I worked for needed re-coding. Unfortunately, they along with my precious ASCII tapes duly went missing somewhere between Bristol Temple Meads and Paddington via British Rail's Red Star delivery service. The excuse for their loss being given at the time was that Temple Meads was undergoing building work and that they were probably under platform four with a whole heap of other rubbish British Rail had built up over the years.

I duly informed the station master of their loss and was told that a British Rail police search of the station was to be undertaken. (Yeh, right!) I think they sent out a Seek and Destroy directive instead of a Search and Retrieve, for they were never recovered.

All these years later and I still think about those damn tapes every time I travel on the train through Bristol Temple Meads. My son, who lives in Coventry is sick of me continually re-telling him the story of them as we pass through the Temple Meads.

Fortunately, for me, perhaps not for you dear reader, I still had the story on seven-inch disks. Another set-back, Linotron's exit stage left from the market in favour of the new all-singing, all-dancing MAC Typesetting System left me no access to typeset them out onto photographic paper reels. Another search, for another boffin, this time to transfer the seven-inch disk to a MAC began in earnest. I was at that time while setting up my own typesetting company thinking of going over to the MAC system. The salesman said he could help. It took him two years though, but good as his word, he managed to find a boffin that had the technology to transfer the disk onto a MAC disk. Unfortunately, computers were moving at such a pace, I went out of business and had to return the MAC, but not before I had transferred the files.

And with no means to read them there they sat. Although Microsoft was moving into the world of the personal computer at that time financially that system was out of my reach. Now with a family to support I didn't have the readies for a new one. Seeing it would be useful to help the children with their homework I managed to secure one second-hand though. An MS DOS. Messing around with it, as you do, I happened across my old disk. Seeing no reason not to, I popped it in – just out of curiosity you understand – and lo and behold up came a whole load of gobbledygook with a little dialog box asking me if I would like to change the format to Microsoft? Well I did. And it did, but to my dismay another load of meaningless gobbledygook came up right across the screen. Out of frustration I scanned down, and down, and down until suddenly hitting the centre of the earth, there it was. Aren't you all lucky readers?

As for the autobiography itself, I would like to say at the outset that it's my story – of a London, seen through the eyes of a young man of sixteen, and not that of others, who may have an entirely different viewpoint and might perceive a contrasting picture to my own. For it is the years between 1961 and 1967. A time that was both exciting and fearful. And one that saw England coming out of its war-time austerities; where change was being led from the front by the young entering into the swinging 'Sixties; where the rest of the country would follow. A time that young people had the pick of jobs, and where fashion was moving apace. Sex was invented for the first time and music was becoming important to a younger generation. For the first time, money, to indulge those excesses was available for those who pursued them.

PROLOGUE

The broadsheet newspaper, the *Daily Mail*, was the bible for compositors during this period. For no other reason than that it carried whole pages of job vacancies in print – just in London. Most were for compositors. It was possible – and I write from personal experience – to scan the *Mail*'s situations vacant while travelling on the London Underground to work; not turn up for your job; but instead get an interview, be offered a job, get taken on, hand your notice in to your old job, starting with the new one the following day.

When I verbally relate this story today, there is a look of incredulity that there was so much work then compared to now. But there was.

The oft time used phrase of the swinging 'Sixties, was that if you remember them you weren't actually there, was more especially aimed at the young middle class that inhabited the art and drama schools, the like of the London School of Economics (as opposed to the London College of Printing and Graphic Arts). The so-called movers and shakers that had money behind them, that attended such privileged institutions, cocked a snoot at those less so enabled; would see them indulging into their created fantasies that bought into their music, fashion, drug and drink-crazed ways of life, that saw the destruction of so much young talent; giving those that survived a secure future and a respectability that they were never entitled. To this day, some of these older 'celebrities' still look down their noses at those of a less social disposition. These people were never part of my world. To quote ex-Prime Minister, Sir John Major's 1990s views on crime: *Society needs to condemn a little more and understand a little less* . . . a line that should have been equally applied to the drug fuelled excesses of rock singers, artists and privileged during the 'Sixties. For my world was of a post-Second World War working class that was emerging from being poor; still not into a class of wealth and privilege. That's not to say that there were not those willing to break their mould of background. Where good job opportunities did exist, and men of foresight made it on their own. And yes, I remember the 'Sixties and it had nothing to do with the chattering class's later interpretation of them – or supposed version. For myself, I openly admit to not being an angel. When I became a journeyman, I had money; and along with my contemporaries, lots of it. I smoked and drank. Often too much for my own good. With little thought that the good times would not last, despite the impending news, must of us put to the back of our minds. That being the constant very real threat of annihilation from a nuclear attack from the Soviet Union. A Cold War was something we had no control over. The *Campaign for Nuclear Disarmament*, Europe's largest single issue peace movement sought unilateral disarmament. Great Britain had the H-bomb but was an incidental power alongside the Soviet Union and the USA that might draw us into a conflict that would not last long for either side. We were on a collision course to world destruction after a failed CIA-backed invasion of Castro's Cuba gave Nikita Khrushchev the opportunity to build a missile base on that island country in the Caribbean under the pretext that it would deter the USA from sending in the military to depose Castro.

There was a thirteen-day stand-off. The world held its breath. It was touch and go, and I say that without fear of contradiction. It's easy to think otherwise; but the fact remained that the then President of America, John F. Kennedy gave the Soviet Union an ultimatum to pull their missiles out of Cuba or a strike would be made against them. These were politically strong words for an American president let alone one that was a Democrat. If his bluff had been called, then a Third World War would have come and gone in less than two hours.

The only thing good about a Third World War would be that a national call-up of the working-classes to defend the freedoms of the upper- would not be on the Government's agenda.

Some took a philosophical approach to death by a nuclear holocaust – that you could only die once; or, you won't know anything about it when it happens – which, was true. But as you get older: as I got older, and had children and grandchildren, one begins to realise a truth. Whatever a person's religion – if religion be the right word – this beautifully created and crafted world came not from nothing, or if it did, it was one hell of a coincidence which I for one cannot buy into. But if you want to accept coincidence then the philosophy is just the same. For humanity and its children must be about the most valuable commodity to have come from nothing: the sanctity of life that can so easily be discarded and disregarded in favour of self-interest; is an affront to whoever or whatever gave it us, will only go so far before we get one hell of a whack from the affronter.

But before that possible outcome of a Third World War, and what was headlined as the 'Bay of Pigs', Cuban missile crisis, the Russian President, Nikita Khrushchev, had the good grace to withdraw his country's missiles from America's backyard in 1962 in exchange for America removing theirs already deployed in Turkey and Italy (not a lot of people knew that), and which became a precursor for a nuclear test-ban treaty in 1963 between the two super powers and the United Kingdom. We all breathed easy – for a time at least. There was no victory gain for either side; and no crowing either. But overall threats didn't go away. There were other occasions; and the genuine feel among my circle of peers was that we would not make old bones; and that it would only be a matter of time before Russian and Chinese troops would be marching down London's Oxford Street with snow on their boots.

Though the fear of a nuclear attack from another nation has largely been put on the back boiler, the threat of a nuclear device being brought to our door by a terrorist brings new fears for a new generation. Let's just hope that *our* Affronter is not pointing a finger in our direction, waving it with cautionary words of, *You're pushing your luck you lot. I'll not warn you for much longer! Sort yourselves out, or I'll replace you with something less intelligent!*

1 – THE LINE IS ON

THE LATE Charles Dickens' wrote:
> 'I am certain that there are not in any ordinary branch of manual dexterity so many remarkable men as might be found in the printing trade. For quickness of perception, amount of endurance, and willingness to oblige, I have found the compositor pre-eminent.'

I am obliged to concur with the eminent fictionist.

The letter arrived. Dear Gilbert Jackson, *it said here*, we are pleased to inform you that you have passed your examination and interview with the Advertisement Production Employers' Federation/London Typographical Society examining board and that you are to present yourself to Messrs. Craske, Vaus and Crampton, 31 Earlham Street, WC2, at 8am on the morning of Monday, 24th July 1962.

I could hardly believe it. The examination and the interviews were all behind me. I was finally to become an apprentice compositor. Not to the general trade but to what was known as an APEF house. This was an unknown before that time as it was not considered the right type of skills environment for an apprentice compositor to learn his craft; but being a shortage of specialising compositors to learn the new trade of ad-setting and reproduction that the London advertising agencies demanded, and with the London College of Printing prepared to make up any short-fall in knowledge, the trade, represented by employers and unions, rescinded.

It had been touch and go as to whether I would get into the printing industry. Having originally passed the entrance exam with the British Federation of Master Printers to be a photoengraver; and they not having any placements until the following year I had in the meantime sat the entrance exam to be a gas-fitter. Having passed their entrance board exam and interview they offered me an apprenticeship. I was about to leave school and take up their wonderful offer when my brother happened to mention this new APEF and their new scheme to make apprenticeships available. Another hurried exam, an interview, quickly followed by an acceptance – and I was the Gas Board's loss. My brother Keith, being a letterpress machine minder working for Odhams Press when not serving the union as an Executive Officer for the National Graphical Association steered me in almost seamlessly where I would earn a grand wage of £3. 19s. 6d.

I lived in Tooting, a suburb of Wandsworth in South London with my mum Ida, my dad Ernie, and sister Christine. Keith, who had just married his fiancée from Putney, Maureen (anyone living close to Wandsworth's Young's Brewery was alright by me), were living a few doors down from us and said that he would take me to work until I had got my own transport sorted out. He had a Lambretta 150LD and it was on that I was to ride pillion on that first day.

It was a bright, cold summer morning when we set off on Keith's Lambretta to head into the capital. I didn't feel the cold that day. I was too excited.

Weaving through London's dense traffic, Keith wearing his Crombie military overcoat with regulation check cheese-cutter cap, with me wearing a camping anorak, which, per my now fashion conscious mates, I was beginning to live in. (I was still hanging onto an idea that I might yet be an Antarctic explorer.) Before I knew it, we were on Waterloo Bridge crossing the River Thames. The Tamesas, to give it its Brittonic Celtic name, is the great divide, where south meets north. On the left as we crossed over was The Royal Festival Hall where I had recently seen Thelonious Monk in concert. I was a bit of a Jazz fan then. Across Waterloo Bridge we reached the Strand and the Aldwych. To the east in the distance was Trafalgar Square where I had been employed on a school summer holiday job working for the Navy League at Admiralty House. The warmth of the early morning sun on the river gave a vapour mist in the middle, its atmosphere sense is with me still. The excitement of going to work that first morning in London, with all its possibilities, was a dream come true.

Keith continued across the bridge, down through the Strand underpass known colloquially as the Drain, where we emerged out into Kingsway. From here it was left turn into Great Queen Street where could be found the Connaught Rooms where business meetings and Masonic gatherings took place. The top of Great Queen Street took you into Longacre and the edge of Covent Garden Market which was also close to the home of Odhams Press and *The Daily Herald*. The only true newspaper for the working classes those days if you discounted the *Morning Star*. The reading of which could have you shot for a Red spy.

Odhams Press was a leviathan of a building with great underground workings where printing presses the size of houses were rooted into the ground before growing up through two or three floors. Enormous warehouses below held forests of paper rolls. Here tankers full of ink with flexible hoses the girth of pythons pumped its blood through valved pipes set into the building's walls. To a boy like me, whose ambition was to become a print worker, the aroma of paper and ink from the inside of the building wafting out was intoxicating. This was what it was all about. You could feel the power of the printed word and for me it indelibly embossed itself into my senses. This newspaper building was, along with others scattered around this part of London, were the bastions of civilised life (not my words): the books, the newspapers, and the communication of ideas of men; it was all here. Even with new technologies it is with me still. Nothing has changed for me; the power of printing lives on in me. When like yesterday's newspaper I become yesterday's story people will walk past the crematorium where I'm making my first and last appearance, they will sniff the air and say to the sage within them: 'Where's that burning ink and paper smell coming from?' And the sage will answer: 'Ah, that's the author being re-cycled at the great paper mill in the sky. In common with all men and newspapers he is . . . tomorrow's fish and chip wrapper: an ephemeral man.'

Keith leaned the Lambretta up against an ink intake valve, pointed me in the direction in which I was to go then saying good luck; 'I'll pick you up at 5 o'clock. Goody, good!'

With my school woodworking apron tucked under one arm; with my mum's dripping and salt sandwich in my hand (wrapped!) I nervously made my way to the place of work that was to be my home for the next six years.

Earlham Street had high industrial buildings with warehouse below both sides of its narrow road. Crossing the junction of Monmouth Street and six other roads this part of London was known as Seven Dials. Here it continued to Cambridge Circus where Charing X Road intercepts Shaftesbury Avenue. It was the main road into the Covent Garden fruit and vegetable market. Craske Vaus and Crampton were three floors up on the edge of the market. It had an art frame factory below and a Fyffes banana ripening wholesaler at street level below. Behind, the Donmar Rehearsal Theatre, today known as the Donmar, apprentices and journeymen would watch actors and actresses learning their lines on the fire-escape steps at its rear. One was the young Barbara Deeks, *aka* Windsor, a *Carry On* film favourite for younger audiences at that time. And not just the young, considering Miss Windsor's acting abilities, as well as many other of her attributes. I don't think those films have lost their appeal even today, with Miss Windsor reaching out to modern day audiences with her appearances in *EastEnders*, one of the most famous soaps in the world, and her becoming a national institution with royalty as well as the public a consequence. Her elevation to that of Dame Barbara Windsor DBE underlining that fact.

There was room to park cars alongside the heating cabinets under the building it was that large. Mind you, you had to share with other less welcome inhabitants. *Tarantulas!* With leg spans the size of dinner plates they would emerge from the roof trusses above when all was quiet. These creatures brought in with the hands of bananas from such exotic places as Colombia were merely brushed off the shoulders of the carriers as more of a nuisance than something deadly. At night-time, it afforded shelter for local meths drinkers and other down-and-outs that couldn't afford the price of a room at the Salvation Army's local doss centre. Thrupence, was not so easily come by when you've nothing, when drink is more important to your soul. A century before it had been the winter quarters for a circus. Here they kept the elephants. I swear blind I could still smell 'em.

In the corner of this car parking space I found a lift. Others were already waiting for it. It was to take me to up to CVC. The initials CVC were affectionately known by the journeymen when speaking of some of the management. On the lines of: Something, Vermin and Crawlers. Can't exactly remember the first word. Probably just as well. Someone pulled open the convoluted metal gates to the lift, and we all ventured in. A smell of rotted fruit accompanied the passengers. Someone hit the one of four lift buttons. None had any indication either by name or number which was which and what floor each represented. Wrongly wired, they were out of a natural sequence. Not that that presented any real problem, as only one of them worked. There was a bang of machinery and a clanking of wheels, a shudder, then the carriage lifted off. I clung to the sides fearing for my life. Another bang came when it reached its destination. The doors were opened, and my two fellow passengers stepped out. Then, just as I was about to do the same, the carriage dropped. My heart skipped a beat, my hand reached out to a handrail inside on one of the lift's sides I desperately clung on fearing a plunge of death to the ground below. What at first seemed like dropping three floors, but was in fact nearer an inch, I breathed a sigh of relief. Someone shouted back, 'It's only taking up the slack of the cable.' I gingerly slid the gate further open to make my escape and leaping the gap shut the gate behind me. The lift banged and this time it did drop. My immediate reaction was that it had come off its pulley, but it was only someone else calling it down.

I stood at the entrance to a long narrow room with double framed-benches lit by strip lights. Three large flat-iron topped tables led down the room. At the end was a large iron riveted sliding door that led into the offices. All about were men wearing woodworking aprons, carrying frames of type, fags hanging from their mouths. Standing at the iron tables they were banging with wooden blocks and mallets. Some had tweezers and steel rules sticking out of their apron pouches at the front. All tooing and froing doing different tasks, which at that time were not only alien to me but made me wonder what I had let myself in for. Then the noise stopped. Some of the men started taking off their aprons and opening cabinets behind their working frames. Putting on their coats they started to leave. *Why were they going home we've only just got here?* I thought to myself. They then went to a clock attached to the wall beside the lift. Here they pulled cards out of a rack beside it, put them into the clock. Then banging a handle on the side, they then put the cards back into their file slots and shouted, *Goody, good!* to no-one in particular, before going to the lift as others were coming out, before being lowered back to the ground to go home. This was the night shift apparently.

I stood nervously not knowing what to expect, but not for long. A short, stockish, balding man wearing an immaculate tonic mohair suit approached me. He looked to be in his forties and had a smile on his face that was infectious. With this disposition of geniality, I instinctively knew that I was in good hands. Hand out to take mine, he said, 'I'm George – George Good, comp room overseer, glad to have you aboard, you must be Gilbert.'

'Err, Gil,' I corrected, 'Gil Jackson.'

'Ah, another Jacko, Gil Jacko, howya! howya! howya! you must be one of the STONEWALL JACKSON'S!'

'Don't think so,' I replied having never heard of them. 'Not in any of my family that's for sure.' But he had already ignored me. He looked to be in his forties and had a smile on his face that was infectious. With this disposition of geniality, I instinctively knew that I was in good hands.

'I'm surrounded by Jackson's.'

He then came back alongside of me and put his arm around my shoulders, 'You come with me, howya! howya! howya!' he said escorting me into the comp room proper. The day-shift men having dispensed with their jackets were settling themselves down for their day's work looked up to see the new distraction arriving. 'Here he is, the other one,' George said by way of a brief introduction. Good morning and hee-haws went up in welcome from the dozen or so journeymen that were to

THE LINE IS ON

be my mentors for the next six years as I was led down the line. Men in their twenties and early thirties, I felt the trepidations of a new boy arriving at his new school being encouraged by a headmaster that had so much knowledge to divest he was overflowing with the enthusiasm of its secrets.

With formal introductions ignored until a need to know, George took me on to his office which was the same as all others in that it also had a bench that became known to me as a frame. Here I was to fill in a piece of paper to verify my name, age and address, next of kin (that sounded encouraging), before George took it away with a passing and a smiling remark of, 'And have you been circumcised? Ha-ha-ha!' But he was not waiting for an answer. Just as well, I was only familiar with the term cavalier or roundhead. He then asked me to wait while he disappeared out through double doors to return with another boy. Bruce, who, we together, were about to share our formative years as apprentices to become men. Here I must say, I was slightly disappointed as I was kind of hoping that I would be teamed up with a guy that had sat through the exams and interviews with, but as it turned out, Bruce was okay. It appeared that we had similar interests: camping, canoeing: the need to buy a shotgun. It was no coincidence that we had been put to work in the same place by the employers' federation. The only differences between us was, he came from Enfield, in north London; and with me coming from south of the river, we had little opportunity to socialise. We shook hands.

'This is Bruce, Wells – as in, BOMBADIER BILLY!'

(He certainly had a penchant for the sobriquet. It was just

a pity neither of us knew what the hell he was on about.)

George called over a man called Dave Pattison, who we were told was the Father of the Chapel (a what?). He was tall, with a dark complexion with black hair to match and carried George's sobriquet of, 'This is, BLACK PAT!' What else? It was his job to explain to Bruce and me what was to be expected of us from the union's point of view. First, there was tea to be made at various times during the day; the men's sandwiches to be bought; and mumping arrangements (mumping – what?). He went on to explain that he was the man to whom we went if we had any complaints or problems. He was the top man on the shop floor union-wise, and union-wise. The power of the printing unions at that time was akin to that of the Dockers and the Miners; their law, was the Word; and BLACK PAT! in this new world was – the word.

When all had been explained to us as to how we were to conduct ourselves in our relationships to the journeymen we went back to George. Here he allotted the pair of us each to a journeyman. As Bruce had already done some basic composing at school it was decided that he would go into the reading room and I to the composing room. Alfie Jackson and his copy-holder, Archie, were to be his mentors for two weeks when we would then swop over. This would go on for six months. So, on that first day, I was allotted George Good as my mentor journeyman and Bruce got Alfie Jackson as his.

2 – THE COMPOSER

HISTORY doesn't exactly record where or when the term compositor emanated relative to one whom sets single letters of lead or wooden type. Printer seems to have been the generic term that encompassed the craft of both setting the type and printing the image from it. Composing music or a composer of music has an altogether different interpretation both easily understood in that they are a creative art form of expression; whereas a compositor is not creating in the same sense. Unless he was also an author or poet producing his works by the means of composing the letters of type as he creates, as opposed to using a quill or pencil. The likely explanation is from the word composite and its Latin derivation compositus, meaning put together of many parts. If, however, you've heard of a compositor and it doesn't match the definition of what I have given here it is because the word is now used for an editor of blue and green screen technology for film and television where images are presented as composite overlays.

'This,' George said opening the palms of his hands in the presentation of his work-station, 'is where compositors' compose. This,' he continued, 'is called a frame. As you can see it's a double slanted-top metal bench. Below, here, are its racks of cases that store the type. Ten-point Grot 150, this'll do.' He bent down and dragged out a case, brought it up to his chest dropping it on the frame with a crash and a blast of dust. There was a lip at the edge of the frame that prevented it sliding onto the floor. 'The case of type that you want is put on the top of the frame, thus – and leans towards the compositor at an angle. Yes?'

My mind wandered off.

'*Yes?*'

'Oh, yeh, sorry.'

He smiled. 'Try and keep up then. *Grotesque*,' he said with a smile, 'from the Italian word grotessca, *not* the English grotty, howa! howa! howa!'

He smiled again at another of his enlightenments.

Grotesque 150, whatever else its hybrid of pretentiousness to Roman arabesque architecture wasn't often used judging by the state of the case holding it. A sans serif typeface that had fallen out of favour was neither enhanced by the bits of ash, fag ends, pieces of ham roll and toffee wrappers found among its contained compartments. Into this I was expected to plunge my young fingers. Grotty both by name and nature. George saw a look on my face of something resembling distain, but never said a word.

He continued. 'Note the angle of the frame. It stops the lines of type from falling over.' He looked around for something, then spotted it, reached over me, and took a metal tray from the end of the frame and held it in front of me. It had a dried ring from a teacup decorating it. '*Galley!*' He then put it to one side of the case.

'Right,' he said patting his pockets, 'Howya! howya! howya! Ah! Here we are.' Finding what he was looking for he pulled out a copy of the day's *Daily Mirror* from his jacket. The paper had been stuffed into his suit pocket with the abandon of someone that had the best in clothes and the worst of environments for sporting them. He opened the paper fanning through the pages before his eye fell on the sports page. He then started to read the article on Tottenham Hotspur, then remembering what he should have been doing continued opening and closing his hands together moving the pages until his eyes fell on to something suitable for copy. 'Here we are, howya! howya! howya! Telstar!' He laid the paper out on the case and began folding it until the article was one piece. I looked over his shoulder.

'Tel what?' I asked.

'Telstar. The *General Post Office*'s communication satellite. The first to be launched in the west. This'll change things . . .'

He wasn't wrong there.

'. . . send telephone calls around the world. Now then, you can set that.'

He opened a drawer in the frame and pulled out a metal tool which looked nothing like I'd ever seen before. 'This,' he said hesitantly, looking for an appropriate anecdote, 'is a stick. And it's called a stick because it's made of metal, howya! howya! howya. No, they were once wood, but now they're metal,' adding as an afterthought, 'except poster sticks, they're still made of wood.' Grinning all over his face at his sense of humour. I said nothing. He coughed and proceeded.

'Right! You take up the stick in your left hand, like so, then pick up the type from the case letter at a time between your thumb and index finger.'

I genuinely meant nothing in my next remark concerning dexterity.

'What if I'm left-handed?'

He looked at me. 'Ah, in that case it goes in your left hand like this, and, no it doesn't, you need a left-handed stick, I'll go and fetch one.'

What passed for embarrassment I said, 'That's OK, I'm right-handed.'

He looked at me as an audience of journeymen had come to watch the entertainment. Then smiling and cocking his head to one side, waved a finger at me to intimate that he knew cheek when he saw it and was appreciative of the subtleness, 'Howya! howya! howya! typical app . . .(muttering under his breath) cheeky little sod, howya! howya! howya. Right, where was I?' Then, looking at the journeymen still standing around watching him commented, 'No work, gents?'

Murmuring and laughing they returned to their frames. He'd seen it all before in his many years in the trade. Loved apprentices and their stumbling ways as he taught them all he knew while watching them grow into journeymen.

I would have liked him to have been around when I eventually became a journeyman; but it was not to be so.

He watched them go, a stern look on his face. He was an overseer with the authority to hire and fire and they knew just how far to push things. He continued with the lesson.

'*Now!* A case of type is made up of ninety-five different compartments. Each one of these houses what are known as the lower case, or small letters; and the upper case, the capital letters, and a section for Arabic figures.'

I studied a figure five he had taken out. 'Thought they were English.'

He wasn't going to be caught a second time today. He smiled nodding. I genuinely didn't know that English figures were known properly as Hindu Arabic numerals.

Originally an upper and lower case were two separate cases, this combination of the two was known as a Californian jobber. More efficient than two cases when it came to advertisement setting. Where large amounts of text needed to be set then two cases would be better as they would hold more, but by that time, indeed quite some time before then, mechanical typesetting had taken hold doing away with large quantities of hand setting. Apart from the boxes containing the alphabet and numerals, there were also those for spaces, extra sorts, such as question marks, dog's cocks, punctuation marks and all the other paraphernalia marks which make up the colourful world of the printed word, and . . .

'What's a dog's cock?' I had asked.

Like all things in this world that could be easier to understand were they to be put into understandable arrangements of order, a case of type with its characters laid out in a haphazard manner might seem to the layman a chance to make difficulties for difficulties sake. The compartments are not arranged in an orderly manner of an A-B sequence for a reason. Well there would be, wouldn't there? How else could you pack in six years of cheap labour if things were that simple. But there *was* a reason as any Scrabble player will tell you.

The letter e, as an example, is in the largest compartment because it is the letter that is mostly used in the English language and has the lowest Scrabble score; an l, a smaller compartment. The result is a conglomeration of compartments all over the case. For instance, the a is next to the r; the o is next to the y; the v, u and t are in a line with each other. Confused? I was.

'*Dog's cock?*' George came back, 'is an exclamation mark'.

He then proceeded to mark each compartment of the case in ink with the letters they contained. I asked why they weren't marked more permanently, to which he replied that the idea was that you looked at the copy not the boxes; that one day I would remember each compartment and would be able to set the type in a stick while carrying on a conversation. I shook my head as if to say, *Don't be so stupid*. Amazingly, whatever the copy, I found later that the amount of effort in going around the case picking characters for the stick is about as efficient as it can get. Fifty years on, having not seen a case of type for thirty of them, I can air set from an imaginary one without thinking.

George continued. 'Lift the character, feel for its nick, it faces forward then put it in the stick like this, reading the copy at the same time.'

Without looking at the case he went at it like a dose of salts, reading the copy lifting each character placing it next to the previous one until he came to the end of the line in the stick. Then, fiddling about with some spaces, brought the line out to the measure that the stick was set to, pulled a brass setting rule from the back of the line, placed it in front of the line of type that he had just set and began another. And another, and another, until in a matter of no time at all, he had a stick full of type. Putting the stick down now, he put his second finger of both hands each side of the lines of type and lifted them clear placing them onto the galley right across the tea stain. Then stepping back to the applause in his head from an invisible audience he said, 'There! Some people would have got a man in to do that.' He then asked me to read the type he had just set.

I looked down at the grey type before me and started to read, then stumbled, the letters were not only upside down, but back to front. I went around the other way to read them. 'No!', George said. 'We read left to right. The fact the type is a mirror image of the word you want to read makes no odds. Reading upside down will allow you to read left to right; and you will learn to read in this manner as well as if you were reading a printed line from a page of a book. (Another skill I've never lost. Useful in meetings when someone has a report in front of him and he's not wanting you to see all of it. Amaze your friends and colleagues.)

'Right,' George continued, 'start setting a character at a time as I did and set your first line of type.'

I took the stick and slowly set the line using the spaces in the lower part of the case until the line was out to the measure of the stick. But the line wouldn't reach to the end, the spaces were not wide enough. George looked at me, then asked me for the time. I turned my wrist over to look at the face of the watch and in doing so forgot that I still had the line of type loose in the stick. I tipped the whole lot out, half onto the floor, the remainder into the case.

George laughed out and was immediately joined in mirth by the other journeymen that had slowly gathered back to watch me. 'Howya! howya! howya!' The first of many stunts that were designed not to catch one out, but to put the subconscious into a change that will prevent it happening again. For a line of type is an object of infinite instability, a living thing, which requires the patience of a saint to overcome the mocking frustration it can inflict. The assembly of which – depending on its content – can be time-consuming in its construction; and be as easily undone if it has a mind. And if it doesn't catch you first time round, it has the memory to abandon the constraints of its restraining chase of quoins if they are not tight on the press, a second. A good line of type wants and needs setting – just the once.

He set another line, then spaced it out.

'You never leave type loose in the stick – it should always be spaced out to its measure, like this.' Someone asked him for the time. He looked up, nodded and with a grin turned the stick over to look at his watch. Miraculously the line stayed where it was. 'See, spaced. Not too tight that it won't come out by lifting, but tight enough to defy gravity.'

He let me set the line again. The same line falling short in the stick he took the stick from me. 'Right. The standard space that we use in ad-setting is the middle or mid, okay?' I nodded. 'If the line doesn't reach the end of the set measure then increase the width of the mid to a thick.' He went to another compartment changing all the mids between the words to thicks. The line got wider, but not enough. 'Next, two thins.'

THE COMPOSER

He repeated the exercise, this time replacing all but one of the thick spaces to two thins, before the line achieved full measure. He then turned the stick over, the line stayed, he put the stick down and removed the line and placed it onto the galley. 'Got it?'

'Think so.'

'Right, listen,' he said, going into rote. 'Order of spaces. Mid, thick, two thins, a thin and a mid, a nut, a thick and a mid, two thicks, one thick two mids. If the line comes very close to measure using mids, then reduce line space to a thin. If the word spacing becomes too much for the look of the text being set, then the word on the end needs breaking and hyphenating. Alfie Jackson, the reader, knows all about hyphenation, he's made a hobby out of it. That and his photography. God alone knows why, but he spends his holidays in the Low Countries visiting type founders. For the moment though, you begin setting that Telstar article. And notice that the first paragraph is set a larger size than the rest, so follow it. I'll be in the reading room if you need me.'

Then he was gone, and I was standing in a composing room in the middle of London on the first day of a six-year apprenticeship with pretensions to becoming a craftsman. A copy of the *Daily Mirror* in front of me, a news item referring to some new technology called Telstar, a case of Grot 150, my stick, my spaces, and the whole of my future in front of me. In the shadow of Johannes Gutenberg and his 1450 42-line Bible; the first book to be produced using movable type. I began setting.

After what seemed like hours of endless fun, George came out to see how I was getting on. I had set the first paragraph 12 point solid justified; the remaining paragraphs I decided as they were smaller would be 10pt also justified. It was 24 ems wide by about 50 ems deep and very precarious in terms of falling over. He looked at my efforts, judged the line lengths and gave me an old-fashioned look, then a smile.

'Looks like the hind leg of a donkey with rivers running though,' he said. (*Rivers?*) 'Still, good effort. We'll tie it up and see what Alfie makes of it (knowing full well that that man wouldn't wait to exercise his vast knowledge of the printed word to one so in need of a proper education print-wise).

'Right, first some page cord. We need to tie it up before proofing it.' He pulled a ball of string from his draw, disentangled a short length then wound several coils of it around four of his extended fingers. Then, taking a loop around his thumb, took the loose end through the loop and bringing it down sharply snapped it before giving me a stern warning. 'Now don't you do that until you know what you're doing. I'll show how to do that some other time. Right, a little knot in the end of the cord, like so, then put the knotted end just before the top corner and start to wind it around the type. When you come to the first wind trap the knot with the second turn, thus.' He went around and around, pulling it tauter at every fourth turn until the cord was used up. Then putting another loop on it, he pulled some tweezers from his pocket, slipped the cord through, and pulled it back to the corner holding 50 ems by 24 ems of single letter type more manageable than it was.

He then went onto explain the trail of string left over was known as the rat's tail, but not why. Taking from his apron a pen-knife, and with a howya! howya! severed the tail of the rat. He then picked up the galley and walked it up the comp room with me following to a small flat-bedded roller affair that I recognised as being like the one we had in our school art department used for printing lino-cut art.

'This is the proofing press, and every morning and afternoon you and Bruce are to clean off all the old ink, clean the rollers, then re-ink it. I'll get someone to show you how you do that tomorrow,' he said now mindful of the sleeves of his tonic mohair jacket and their proximity to black ink. 'Place the job on the bed of the press.' He angled Telstar onto the bed and with a swift move whipped it off the galley and into position. He then picked up the hand roller and went over the ink plate with it, lifting it then letting it spin before bringing it back down again. 'That's so we get a good even inky roll over the type.' He then rolled the plate again, catching the cuffs of the tonic mohair suit as he brought it back, before remarking quietly to himself, '*Bollocks!* . . . It's a good idea to keep your sleeves rolled up while you're doing this.' He then rolled his suit sleeve up too late before continuing. 'Right, now with the roller, not too coated with ink . . .' (it wasn't, most of it was on his sleeve jacket) '. . . roll it over the type. Then pick up a piece of proofing paper, this is newsprint, place it neatly in the middle of the job, and pull the rollers over it.'

The rollers went over, but unfortunately, there was a small dollop of ink on its rubber surface which stuck to the newsprint lifting the paper from the type taking it around its rollers, tearing it in half. George began to pick the paper off the rollers which had now wound itself nice and tight around the second roller. He forced himself to grin, aware now that others were probably watching. He took his tweezers out and tore at it bit by bit until he had removed it. He wasn't wrong, the inevitable audience had gathered again. A comic or entertainer would pay a small fortune for a bottle of what George had that could pull a crowd. They came in droves those journeymen, and George the Entertainer played up to them, the situation getting worse by the minute the more he considered the problem. And as the sun slowly sunk in the west his very expensive hand tailored tonic mohair suit began to look more and more sticky black in comparison to its previously grey sheen. 'Howya! howya! howya!' he said half in desperation and half in anticipation that he would soon have it sorted. The audience was not going to go away until he had cracked the problem removing every piece of paper from that roller. They all had galleys of type in their hands, supposedly waiting to be proofed for reading. George might have thought conspiracy, but he couldn't prove it. I thought coincidence, but I *was* naive, he wasn't, and could say nothing. He was stuck with the situation with an inevitability that his very expensive suit was ruined.

Having removed the last vestige of paper, he put a fresh piece of newsprint on Telstar, this time wiping the rollers clean making sure there were no more sticky surprises waiting for him, ran the rollers over again, took off the newsprint and there was the perfect impression of Telstar – my first time in print.

George picked up a conical shaped can with a peppered top, sprinkled the contents over the type (carbon tetrachloride), and with a rag cleaned the ink off. Job done. *Some people would have got a man in to do that*, a voice echoed in my head.

You know when you've been told not to do something by someone . . . like, you see a sign on a lamp post saying: Wet Paint Do Not Touch. Well . . . you've just got to put your finger in it, haven't you, just to check like? Or, Keep Off The Grass, you've just to dab a shoe on the edge of it having ascertained that no-one is watching you; or, Do Not Feed The Ducks. You surreptitiously pick a small piece of bread from your sandwich and throw it in the water; or, never mind you get my drift. Well, George, and this trick of breaking page cord using his hands gnawed at me like a rat at a rope. Something akin to putting off getting up out of a warm bed on a cold winter's night to go to for a wee.

    So, taking up a roll of page cord when no one was about, I roughly worked out what George had done, the principle, if you like. Rolled several turns of cord around my hand, locked a piece of the cord against itself and with a deft tug attempted snapping the cord.

    It was two days before my hand had recovered from the tightening of that cord. Its friction burned itself deep into my skin, leaving nasty wheals. The result of not putting enough downwards pull to snap the cord against itself, instead it had chosen to bury itself into my young flesh in ringlets.

3 – THE READING ROOM

CONTRARY to popular opinion a printing reading room is not where journeymen go to drink tea and read the paper. Nor is it a place for them to write out betting slips or have a doss, have rows, raise one's voice, or otherwise make yourself disagreeable demanding that the reader is wrong and that is not how it was done where he worked before. It is a cell for reverence where knowledgeable discussion on how a particular point of order of grammar should be interpreted, words are spelt correctly, or how the compositor could improve the look of the work he has presented to the reader by judicial changes of word spacing and its cousin, interlinear line spacing. Surely, such a sanctity for the betterment of the printed word, openly discussed with compromises from all parties concerned would be peace on earth.

Friend, you may be standing on sacred ground, but you are about to have your balls eaten for breakfast in defiance of any of the above.

'Off to the readers,' George said, purposefully marching down the comp room with me in tow, while I was wondering what all the fuss was about. He grabbed the *Daily Mirror* copy of the Telstar news item from the frame's copy holder with one hand at the same time placing the galley on the frame with not the loss – out of somewhere in the region of 1500 characters and spaces – of one letter. Now that's magic, I thought.

THE READING ROOM

The reading room was close to the comp room and contained a reader by the name of Alfie Jackson (no relation), and a copy holder by the name of Archie. His surname escapes me, but his character hasn't. Archie had a dirty brown handkerchief hanging out of his top jacket pocket that was hanging over the back of his chair. He liked his Frybourg & Treyer snuff did Archie. Fingering a pinch between forefinger and thumb he would show it into each nostril sniffing aggressively the brain accelerant creating an almighty sneeze of proportions guaranteed to eject the eyeballs from their sockets of a lesser mortal. This he would do half a dozen times a day.

Alfie himself neither took snuff nor smoked. A small well-dressed balding man, he would not bat an eyelid at his copy holder's addiction. His stiff upper lip taking Archie and his habit for what he was to get him through his day. For reading aloud, although achievable with practice, is not easy, the act needing both clear dulcet tones and concentration. For Archie with his ability to read in a tone of voice acceptable to Alfie, hardly needed to announce the punctuation marks that accompanied the copy. His lowering and raising of voice, the slight, almost imperceptible to the ear of anyone overhearing him; the interlude between punctuation was an art few can master. Two unlikely characters working in tandem was close to a duet of musicians.

Alfie Jackson's passion, as George had pointed out to me earlier, was the printed word; and for that passion he sometimes had to suffer. He was wasted in ad-setting. A man better suited to typographical study at the British Museum

Library. He collected examples of fine printed books, not to read, but to study their typography, layout and colour. He recognised typefaces like some people football players. As an apprentice, I later realised, I was fortunate indeed to have this man around to give me an appreciation of the printed word; the look of a page of text being crafted lovingly, as opposed to merely being set. It is unfortunate that the Alfie's of this world tend to be the butt of jokes and derisory remarks to those that should know better; but there it is. As head reader, he always had the upper hand when it came to the last word. As the saying prophesises,

> *True, This! —*
> *Beneath the rule of men entirely great*
> *The pen is mightier than the sword. Behold*
> *The arch-enchanters wand! — itself is nothing! —*
> *But taking sorcery from the master-hand*
> *To paralyse the Cæsars, and to strike*
> *The loud earth breathless! — Take away the sword —*
> *States can be saved without it!*

And Alfie could wield a mighty doubled-handed green pen whenever the occasion arose to any journeyman who thought he knew better when it came to the finer points of typography.

As overseer, George's relationship with him could at times become fraught. If Alfie stood his ground over a point that George, following the customer's instructions, he insisted he adhere to. I've seen George fly into a rage over such finery that Alfie did not agree with; returning to the comp room having not quite got the better of the man his face red with anger although knowing he agreed with him, nevertheless had to insist that the customer is always right. The customer's in these cases happened to be some of the top advertising agencies in the world; with copy writers, no doubt close to being academic artisans themselves, had to follow modern trends of slick-speak; no doubt not liking what was being asked of them either. As a point of order, it's the 'law' that a compositor must follow a customer's copy 'out of the window'; then, the reader's mark whether he agrees with the customer or not, must stand. For although the reader is the last arbiter: the referee: the umpire: it's the customer what pays the wages.

Alfie looked up from his desk, and with the demeanour of sternness and single mindedness, pointed to the in-tray with his green pen, cast me the look of a man that had been in better places, and carried on with the job of struggling to listen to Bruce reading to him, while Archie, enjoyed an opportune tea break listened. 'Full point, not full stop. Cap C, then the word! *How many more times must I repeat myself?*'

He was not taken with being interrupted.

'This is Gilbert,' George said announcing me. Alfie nodded, said nothing, and carried on. George seeing his mood with Bruce let him have his space. Putting his hand on my shoulder he ushered me out. I later learned that Alfie's affectionate sobriquet *was* Pickwick; its lesser, *Piss-quick*; spoken in either hushed or harsher tones usually after that point of typographical opinion with journeymen aforementioned. While Archie, was Alfie's Nathaniel Winkle.

4 – DISTRIBUTING

I LOOKED at the reading room proof of my attempt at setting my first job. Covered in ink marks it gave the impression of a spider having stepped into a pot of green ink, got drunk, and had used it as a pavement for its journey home. 'Good, Lord!' was the only comment I could make fearing that I was about to be sacked for total incompetence.

George smiled, clicked his tongue. 'It's not as bad as it looks. Alfie can be a bit enthusiastic. Still—'

He went over the proof, marking what he thought might be encouraging suggestions. 'Lowercase e in Təlstar was upside down, office as in Post Office should carry a capital O, wrong fonts spread generously through the proof . . .' He looked at me, '. . . hardly your fault, I suppose he's just pointing it out. Seems to be quite a few general spelling mistakes. This one here for instance.' I looked over his arm. 'Lester as in Square: should read Leicester; and here, Satelite should be two ll's.' He was beginning to go red in the face. The rest of the proof was covered in other marks that were beyond me, like insert 1 point here and delete 1 point out of there, and visually space through the word TELSTAR. It went on. I could tell that George was beginning to take on the look of a man that was being subtly told to proverbially, 'go suck eggs', when it came to the training of an apprentice – and he was not going to have any of it!

Alfie Jackson – all this time – sitting on what George liked

DISTRIBUTING

to call his 'arrogant laurels' made a casual wander out of the reading room on the pretence of speaking to a journeyman on some other matter, having done so, walked passed George and me, an expression of having done his job, take it or leave it attempted to go back into the reading room under some predisposition of haughty rank. He might have wished that he had let sleeping dogs lie.

George collared him. *'ALFIE!'* He said his name with a commandment and a wave of his finger. Alfie, for his part, an expression of typographical superiority on his face turned, not unexpectedly, ready to justify every mark of his green pen. For this was the man that had made a correction to *Webster's*.

Now we all know that Americans cannot speak English; that they take what we would politely call – and I use the word loosely – a sloppy approach to their true Mother tongue in some mistaken belief that they themselves have somehow improved its diction. Wrong! We would be wise to think again. They are every bit as literate as their Motherland. Authors the like of Steinbeck, Beecher-Stowe, King, Updike, Lee, Roth, and Robinson, to mention but a few, would soon put paid to any such misapprehension. As for *Webster's*, the American equivalent of the *Oxford English*; and the likelihood of finding a mistake just as unlikely was their spellers Bible. However, Alfie, had picked up on a point of order and had written to them explaining his justification for their undoubted error and was expecting a reply someday soon on the lines of a, *Thank you, for pointing that out to us. Of course, you are quite correct, how could we have overlooked the inappropriate application of such a word in its transitive state*. George was nodding his head at him now, '*A word!* If you, please.'

George sent me on a mission to the type store on some pretext. But I made sure I was still within earshot, as was the rest of the comp room.

'What'd you think you're playing at. Just look at this proof. I told you to check it for literals, with just the odd mark for the benefit of a little learning. I never asked you to go over it as if it was an example of typographical excellence with the British Museum Library in mind.'

Alfie stood there, the haughty expression still on his face; made some remark to the effect that he was not going to lower his standards for an apprentice.

'*This* is his first day,' George bellowed. 'Was it your intent to teach him everything there is to know about the finer points of print from a poxy newspaper cutting. *Get out of here!*'

Alfie turned, muttered something on the lines of lowering standards; and ad-setting being a poor enough place as it was.

That remark was a red rag to a bull. George didn't need lessons on what Alfie conceived as the lowering of standards.

'Back in your box you insufferable moron!' Alfie did as he was told. But ten minutes later, when the two had to converse over some other typographical detail it was as if nothing had happened. And I learned two lessons that day: Never hold a grudge (well, not for too long). And that: Pride goeth before destruction, and an haughty spirit before a fall.

When later in my apprenticeship, I happened into the reading room where a collection of reference books and

DISTRIBUTING

dictionaries had been put together by Alfie; *Webster's,* not being the least of them caught my eye. American–English variations intrigued me, and how easy the spelling of a word, like for instance the English, aeroplane with its American equivalent, airplane; or the idiom – and I quote here from *Fowler's*, for the sake of expediency and authentication – the English, leave well alone, and its American counterpart, also leave well enough alone. Would any one man be wise enough to question, if he was not sure of his ground, the complexities of the two languages with these two statements alone argue the toss, unless, to the degree of Fellow of English at Warwick University; or a Professor of Idiocy (and far from it for me to suggest thin lines here), at The School of Suffering Adequacies. No, only from the latter. Under the word, eggplant had been signalled in dots of green ink a stet mark in the margin. The word aubergine had been lined through with a delete symbol next to it. *A-hem*. Amen to that. Nice try.

After correcting Telstar for the fourth time, having kept missing marks that Alfie had put on subsequent proofs. 1st, 2nd, 3rd, and Final; pulling a proof for my folder, I was to 'diss' the type back into its case.

'This is the quickest way to learn the lay of the case,' George stated adding with a smile, 'and a more boring job I've yet to find.

By the way, where did you get those red weals on your hand from?'

* * *

Distributing, diss or dissing is what is done to the set job to recover the type when it is finished with. Recycling might be a better word, but the term hadn't been invented back then. Assuming it hadn't been flattened beyond recognition in the foundry (more on that later). It is well known among compositors that there is always work in the comp room, and 'dissing' is to what they are generally referring. Of course, there was not always the time to put the type back straight away. Ad-setting and reproduction in the world of advertising was always busy. Lines of type, odd characters would find their way to the top of one's frame to gather dust until work dropped off when they would be dealt with. Assuming the journeyman didn't have more important tasks to attend to like reading the paper or making out betting slips. If everyone was out of work and the overseer deemed it was necessary to clear this backlog of type, then a combined effort by all would ensue.

Then there would be a general bustle of cases being pulled out, type dropped in, then pushed back. Some typefaces alluded some in what they were. Not for any other reason than with the infinite number of faces that were similar; bearing in mind that a compositor would not be working with all of them, not all of the time, memories fade. Apart from George and Alfie there was one other man that was the Google man of the day when it came to typeface recognition, and that was the store man. His job was to buy-in type and organise the borrowing of it from other companies when it was not always economical to buy. He would check out cases to see if they were running low adding to them with new packets he kept in a storeroom. Being constantly looking at all types, all day, his familiarity with the name of the face became second nature. The consequence was that he was constantly being asked a type face that was unfamiliar to journeymen and apprentices alike. Funny thing was apprentices were able to take in the look and recall the type face better than some journeymen. Whether it was their keenness, or young brains being receptive, I couldn't really say. Having said that though, some typefaces did present problems in that a type founder may have produced a face similar to another. It may be something as small as the descender of a lowercase y or the lower stroke of a capital R. And if the line of type that you were trying to replace had neither of these to substantiate the name of the face, then short of asking someone or going to both cases and comparing two characters between fingers usually did the trick. But still, mistakes could be made and a case may wind up being distributed by the wrong typeface, even the wrong size, making it a nightmare for the next man that came along to use the case only to find that as he was setting he was constantly having to discard letter after letter from his stick. The only answer then was to empty the entire case into a bin for melting down and replacing the contents with new packets from the store.

As for dissing itself, George was not wrong. It was *bloody boring!* But it was the quickest way for an apprentice to learn the lay of the case.

Of course, I quickly worked out the best way to tackle this sometime mundane task. The sound of separate characters of type being dropped into their appropriate boxes in the case can be duplicated without having to actually – diss them. By hanging a mutton space on a piece of page cord. A trick needed to be learned very early on if one's sanity is to be preserved. In earshot of your journeyman or overseer, but not of course in sight, the apprentice drags this 'mutton' around the case banging it against the side of the boxes as he goes. With skill and the look of intelligence he can fool anyone. Anyone that is, except George Good, who, if he cottoned on to what you were about, would creep up behind you and whack you around the ear with a rolled-up *Daily Mirror* he had dragged from his tonic mohair suit pocket. 'Howya! Howya! Howya! Apps eh! Hu!' he would say with a smile before walking on his way.

Fake 'dissing' was carried out with impunity at the London College of Printing in Stamford Street. The silt at the bottom of the Thames underneath Waterloo bridge will be the last remaining lead mine when the world's resources finally run dry. This being the normal way home for apprentice compositors living north of the river. Upstairs on the bus, window down, handfuls of lead type in clutched hands, drawn from bulging pockets, cascading from the bus into the river like so much ground bait. And that must have been going on for decades since the foundation of the college until its removal to the Elephant and Castle in 1966. Passed on from generation to generation of apprentice compositors. Mind you, that was tolerated and treated as a one of those things, but woe betide anyone getting caught doing the same to founders type.

The only thing that this form of 'dissing' into the river doesn't do, is of course to allow the type to be reused again.

DISTRIBUTING

There is only one other thing that you can do to type that is no longer required, and that is to put it in the lead scrap bin. This would be collected by a metal salvage company on a regular basis where it would be melted down, analysed, where if necessary additional alloys would be added before being re-cast into ingots and returned.

Telstar took me several hours to 'diss' and George watched over me on that first occasion. Of course, he knew the correct way to do the job by saying the words as you go. That way there was no need to look into your hand to see what character was to go into what box. It could go in almost without thinking.

In those first few months of my apprenticeship, as indeed for the rest of my time, I felt a sense of well-being. And even though at the bottom of the print ladder – grown-up. A part of something traditional and right. Going home at the end of the day; in the lift with that smell of fermenting fruit, printing ink and molten lead in my nostrils; men calling out the familiar sound of not goodnight, or goodbye, or even cheerio, see you tomorrow, but our own words. *Goody! Good!* When I asked my brother why no-one said goodbye or good morning, he told me it was from the habit of night workers coming and going in and out all hours where morning or night was often in doubt.

5 – CLEANERS AND TEA-BREAKS

LES was a quiet, well-mannered man of about fifty. Introducing himself to me later in that first week he asked me if I wanted anything from the shop.

'What sort of shop?' I asked.

'Sandwich shop,' he replied, 'you know, grub for tea break, bacon sandwiches, egg, that sort of thing.'

Thinking I could do with a change from mother's salt and dripping sandwiches I said I would. Why not, I was after all, earning money now.

'Well, what'd you want?' he said.

'Cheese roll – do they do cheese rolls?'

He pulled a strip of paper from his pocket that had a list of names on it. He wrote Gil – cheese roll.

'Five pence,' he said, 'where's your cup?'

'*Cup!*'

'For tea.'

'Haven't got no cup.'

'Better have one then. I've probably got an old one outside for you to use if you want it.'

Not particularly fancying the idea of using someone else's old cup I said no thanks, adding that perhaps he could get me one while he was out.

He wrote down cup next to cheese roll.

CLEANERS AND TEA-BREAKS

Black Pat came over as Les walked away.

'You've met Les then?'

'Yeh.'

'Good, we'll work something out between you without it interfering with your training too much. Everything alright? George looking after you? He's alright, isn't he?'

'What will we have to do then?'

'I think the best thing that you can do is for you and Bruce to go with Les for a couple of days and he'll show you the ropes. I'll clear it with George.'

'Okay.'

'Yeh, smashing.' I said.

He looked at the piles of pied type on the galley.

'Made a bit of a mess of that.'

'Yeh.'.

'Not to worry, you'll get the hang of it. Lads treating you alright?'

'Bit of ribbing, that's all.'

'You'll get used to it, you're a London apprentice now, the lowest form of life in an ancient trade! You'll get all the shit, and all the kicks. You'll get it from them in fun, and you'll get it from them when they're having a bad day. And don't try and answer back. You've to take it. It's part of the job you're growing into and the sooner you learn that the better off you'll be.' He could see the worried look on my face and I think he wondered if he had said too much. 'Don't you worry though; I'll see that things don't go too badly for you. See it through and the blokes will eventually respect you. You'll be among friends that will not let you down. It's a test, that's all. Okay.'

He patted my shoulders with his big hands.

'Yeh, course,' I said wondering what on earth was to befall me. Dave nodded and turned as someone called after him.

'Right there, Jimmy,' he called across to a small, lumpish man that had an impish look about him. Jimmy nodded.

'Tea up, lads! It was Les coming down the comp room gangway; a trolley with a tray of empty cups at one end, and an enormous steaming teapot at the other.

Journeymen started to go to the middle of the comp room where Les stood. He placed cardboard boxes full of bags onto one of the steel tables. Fitting them among various squares of iron containing type, assortments of wood called furniture, and pictures called half-tones tacked onto bases of lead, all in various stages of having something done to them. The journeymen collected their teas and sorted through the cardboard box before taking them up to a section of the comp room that contained several frames in an open plan arrangement. The steel table that resembled a billiard table without pockets or felt was in fact called a stone and turned out to be another chore at the end of the day.

'That's yours,' Les said to me, pointing to a blue mug with the word STRYCHNINE on its side; 1/6d you owe me, pay me Friday if you like.'

I thanked him and searched for my cheese roll.

Bruce joined me from the reading room, along with Alfie and Archie.

'Where'd we go?' I asked Bruce.

CLEANERS AND TEA-BREAKS

'Over there with the others, I suppose.'

Dave called across.

'Over here you two.'

Alfie and Archie collected their tea and retired back to the reading room for their twenty minutes.

We looked round for somewhere to sit. Dave suggested we pull a case half out of a frame and sit on that. Some of the men had already done that while others were sitting on high stools. Jimmy, the little imp, was sitting on some steps that led into the type storeroom. Behind him was the store man. We pulled our cases out and sat down.

'Not like that, you'll break the bloody thing, pull another out from below it to give it some support.' I looked for the source of the voice. A face appeared from behind a copy of the broadsheet *Daily Mail*, and as quickly went back behind it with the expression of 'bloody apps on it'. It was Kenny the store man. An older man than the rest, that did not appear to have enjoyed good health.

Now, the case that I had just sat was on a level comfortable and in line with one's God-given cushion. I put my tea on the capital section of the case. The boxes of the caps were better able to give support to a cup than the lower. So to get the case out from below – the one I was sitting on – necessitated me to first lift off of the case, turn round to face the frame, pull the case out from below it to half the top one's width to give the necessary support. Unfortunately – and you have to learn by experience in this world – such is the result that upon lifting my backside, the case had a mind, albeit ever so slight a thought, to make a snap upwards back into its original position. Now you remember, you know the bit about where I'd put my teacup. That's right, you're ahead of me, the teacup jumps slopping sugary tea into the case. If you're lucky and you don't take sugar, it's not so serious. If on the other hand you do, as I do, every character that's come into contact with the liquid needs to be taken out and cleaned with paraffin. Mine? Oh, mine. Mine was an apprentice's cup of tea. A cup that knew instinctively that it was not in the hands of an artisan – the whole issue went over flooding K to X before rolling onto the floor and shattering. Never do things by half me.

Oh, God, I thought to myself in panic. Bruce saw what I had done and immediately collapsed in silent laughter. The kind of laugh that you are forced to make when you're not supposed to. The kind of laugh that always reminds me of the time that I was back at school; when the deputy headmaster, at morning assembly, was extolling the virtues of exercising one's bowels before coming to school in the mornings. Not in a sense of fun, but in serious, 'This is no laughing matter, Jenkins, see me after assembly.' Boys sneaking looks at each other, heads about to explode, holding mouths and noses with their hands and anything else that they could close their orifices with. Brains trying to exit their temples. The inevitable sound of farting popping off all around the hall being made by individuals reaching the deputy head's ears as a roar, says again, 'It seems that I have to repeat myself: *THIS IS NO LAUGHING MATTER!*' before the whole assemblage falls into uncontrollable hysteria. That was where Bruce was heading now, along with his own tea and brains.

'*B-L-O-O-D-Y 'E-L-L!* we got a right pair 'ere aint we?' *The Daily Mail* said before returning to his paper muttering. 'You two are going to have to sort that lot out, I'm not doing it.'

'I couldn't 'elp it,' I said out loudly. That would not be the last time I said those words.

Dave sprang to my aid. 'Go see Les, get a cloth and clean it up before it goes sticky.'

This gave me the opportunity to exit from the situation. Bruce quickly followed. Disappearing around the corner, out of the comp room we both went into a full bellow of laughter. Kenny the store man, with the mere hint of a smile reassumed his reading of the sits vac column in the *Mail* – the then Bible for vacancies for compositors that could go to four columns such was the demand for such craftsmen. But it was more from habit than he seeking a new job.

After tea break, I continued setting another piece of copy George had found for me. By lunchtime I had set four paragraphs, and I couldn't help noticing while doing so that there was a sticky treacly substance in the quad box. I had not been the first to spill tea into a case.

Some people can be cruel when it comes to the working lives of people, they consider below them in status. Such was Les's demeanour. He had the habit of getting the odd thing wrong like putting the wrong amounts of sugar into cups. This would encourage some to 'have a go at him' often reducing him to near tears, as I saw on more than one occasion. Not all compositors were compassionate with their fellow man. Woe betide George catching them putting someone down without good reason; he'd have their guts for garters. Les would get over it. But not everyone did. Some weren't so strong.

Albert, his replacement went out and drowned himself in a pond alongside the Houses of Parliament one night. It appears that he'd been, like many, in the army during the Second World War. Prior to his discharge, he'd been seconded to the infamous German Prisoner of War camp known as Auschwitz, to care and feed – prior to some sort of repatriation – many of the tens of thousands of Jews, gypsies, people of differing sexual persuasions, men, and women and children from the fringes of Europe, that had survived the gas chambers of some despot's attempt to conquer the world in his image. Albert had said to me that while there he had seen human beings that had been reduced to carry out appalling acts against others of their own kind just so their captives would be placated into thinking that their policies of genocide were right and that not all deserved to be treated as human. No man, Albert had said to us, whatever race, or religion, had the right to put himself above his fellow creatures.

His suicide may have had nothing to do with anyone picking on him in particular, it might merely have been one straw too many. His words did influence me though. History has taught us that going to war to prevent genocide against others will be conveniently forgotten. As will the will to act against consequent aggressors.

In the case of Les, a man that few saw not as one that had

been reduced to making tea and carrying out general cleaning duties for our betterment; with no other worth, eventually left returning to what he had once been. Few realised that he spoke several languages and was in fact a lecturer at London University in the classics before he had had a nervous breakdown. It's a funny old world, you just don't know who's who, what, or has been, as we all bump along through life.

6 – THE BINDING CEREMONY

MY INDENTURE was signed the Eleventh Day of January One Thousand Nine Hundred and Sixty-Three at Stationers' Hall, London. Stationers' Hall is the traditional home of liverymen within the City of London of many callings, and not just printers and compositors.

For an apprentice to become a master and set-up a press in the City of London in the 16th century he needed both the Freedom of the Company and the Freedom of the City of London. For that to happen he either had to be the son of a Freeman; or having served and completed an apprenticeship to a Freeman; or by redemption or purchase of the title.

In the printing industry, the Stationers' managed the restricted rights to sell and print books – an entitlement normally reserved for those with a Royal licence – as well as exercising powers over patents, and copyright. Bibles, law, and schoolbooks under these patents and copyrights. This was where the money was, and for the wealthy that could afford those Patents they had it made. A Queen's Printer's Patent for the Bible cost one printer £3,000 in 1580 to set up his business. Without a vast financial resource, even a master printer would be hard pushed to get his press moving. His only option would be to sub-contract for a printer that already had the patent to publish his own work. The result was that the printer had to wholesale his publications to the book-sellers at a price that was

THE BINDING CEREMONY

either low or non-existent. (No change there then.)

After years of journeymen printers having served time as apprentices wanting to set-up as masters; and having these curtailments was tantamount to working against cartels. The ruling court of the time was the Courts of Star Chamber and High Commission. The new boys were having to fall into piracy and the printing of seditious material. And as one Roger Warde said addressing himself to the Courts of Star Chamber on a charge of printing piracy in 1582:

> 'A very small number in respect of the Company of Stationers, Printers, having gotten all the best books and "copies" [sic] to be printed by themselves by privilege, whereby they make books dearer than otherwise they would be. And having left very little or nothing at all for the residue of the Company of the Printers to live upon, unless they should work under them for such small wages as they of themselves please to give them, which is not sufficient to find such workmen and their families to live upon, whereby they through privileges enrich themselves greatly and become, some of them great purchasers of lands and owners of large possessions.'

Roger Warde was a brave man as The Courts of Star Chamber and High Commission had the power – short of the death penalty – when it came to trying cases of sedition or piracy to have miscreants flogged, or their ears removed. As for seditious material, you could be branded on both cheeks with the letters SL (seditious libeller). It is not known what Roger Warde's fate was, but as he managed to sell and print books after that date – becoming known as the Elizabethan printer – we must assume he got away with it. Powers were passed to the Court of the Stationers' to oversee copyright patents, numbers of printing offices. In 1641 the Courts of Star Chamber and High Commission were abolished. There being no alternative sanctions against printers, they flourished.

I recently saw a copy of one of Roger Warde's books in a rare book sale room. It was priced at £6000. By 1695 the powers of the Stationers' Company themselves diminished. Printing became a free for all with the advent of the English Civil War in 1638, such was the need for religious and political pamphlets. That was, until the restoration of the monarchy in the name of Charles II. With the execution of his father, no doubt very much on his mind; he, not wanting to take any risks with seditious material, a re-enactment of the regulations was revived, before it was allowed to fall back again on certain conditions. A master printer could then set up either in London or in the provinces and print what he liked (a message for social media providers coming up), provided it wasn't libellous, seditious or obscene.

My indenturing ceremony took place several months after the start of my apprenticeship and was to last five years and ten months (the apprenticeship, not the ceremony). Attended by all the apprentices that were in the new APEF/NGA Alliance, together with their parents – in my case – dad. What with them and all those dignitaries on the top table it was quite a crowd and an occasion.

After a pre-amble by the president, then his vice, then Lord knows who else that wanted to have a say, we bare foot, and bare shouldered (*Bare foot! Bare shouldered!* Sorry made that bit up, thinking about the Masons), one by one we got up to read the Oath of Allegiance. All went swimmingly until it was my turn.

Standing to attention, my Oath in hand, I was ready to read before the assemblage when my dad cupped his hand over his mouth and whispered in my direction.

'Your fly buttons are undone!'

I didn't hear him at first, although I thought I heard him speak I think I thought it might have been him coughing. Then he spoke again. This time I got it and it was like a bombshell in the quietness. With me holding my breath about to start reading my lines, I looked hesitantly to one side, not wanting to draw any more attention at this distraction than I had to. I whispered back. '*What?*' No one seemed to notice my speaking. I think I got away with it.

Dad raised his voice this time by a semi-tone.

'Pardon. I said your flies are undone.'

I shook my head.

'Still can't hear you, what did you say?'

'I said . . .'

He looked around at the assembly. Then in a loud whisper that he must have thought would not be heard repeated.

'*YOUR FLIES ARE UNDONE!*'

All about heads turned. I looked down. Oh, God. The safety pin, that had been used as an emergency earlier was wide open, threatening a nasty injury at any moment. *Can someone please open a hole in the earth for I wish to be swallowed up.*

Stationers' Hall is not an arena for flippancy of dress. And this *was* an important occasion. The hall full of parents, employers' and other such aforementionables, watching their prodigies and cheap labour, depending on your aspect, being indentured to the printing industry in such auspicious surroundings gave an air something akin to a coronation, or at least a Lord Mayor's day swearing-in ceremony.

With as much of my shirt and y-fronts tucked away as it was possible to do with one hand without looking like a pervert I proceeded with the printed card. My voice shaking, I hesitantly began reading the words before me, before breaking into a gallop to finish them as quickly as my little legs would carry me with barely a sound that was likely to be construed as the words on the card:

I clearly understand (pace increasing) the permanent and binding nature of this Contract and (tearing along now) undertake faithfully to serve my Master for the full period of the Indenture (almost one word). I deliver this as my act and deed.

I looked around, smiled, and quickly sat down. Then it was my dad's turn.

Now, just a brief word about my father. To give you some insight as to the nature of the man. He was born in Lambeth 8th November 1908. Not quite within the sound of Bow Bells – unless a strong north-easterly carried its peels – to be ascribed as a Cockney, but within a gnat's cock. He was one of nine siblings.

Too young for the First World War and a smidgen too old for the Second he had escaped. Although having said that, as an electrical engineer and part-time barber, he was what was known as reserve occupation. Not that barbers were particularly needed; but engineers, however, were. The government of the day suggested his skills would have been of more use to a country at war than getting shot at overseas. After a day in the factory working a lathe, he took up his night-time hobby of standing on its roof watching for incendiaries for the company's fire-watch team. A highly dangerous occupation. For London was not best placed for such diversions. For although he and his fellow compatriots were able to direct the regular fire brigade to potential fires, Hitler got his own back on him by bombing out the barber shop that he and his mate had in Streatham before the war; and which he would hopefully return after.

He was a small man but had a raging temper when roused. Persistent though. He spent some years wooing my mother, who, *apparently*, seeing nothing much in him, but enough to fall pregnant with my brother, conjoined a hasty marriage to him.

He used to play a banjo uke with his mate in pubs for beer money. The pair of them, straw-hatted with striped blazers looking like characters out of the book *Three Men In A Boat* made it no further than the saloon bar, let alone the London Palladium.

With a grounding in performing, his own father made him sing in pubs when he was a little boy of three, then take the money from the hat that had been passed around, sent the boy home with a clip around the ear, then drank the night away before returning home himself to beat his wife senseless. There was a lot of it about. They were known as the good old days.

My dad, naturally, became a bit of a disciplinarian when it came to his own children, but he never knocked our mother about – but by the Lord Harry, did they have some hum-dingers of rows. Sunday lunch time was the usual venue, ending with a bowl of custard being thrown up the wall.

They never had holidays together until they retired and settled down a bit. He preferred the countryside, Bournemouth, and Eastbourne; she, Southend, Brighton, the bright lights and jellied eels. My sister holidayed with her, and I with my dad. I remember one occasion we were at breakfast in an Eastbourne boarding house and I had drunk five cups of tea:

'*Dad! Dad!* How many cups of tea have you had, *dad? Dad!*' His head buried in the *Daily Telegraph*, a Senior Service hanging from his lips looked up then carried on reading. 'Dad, how many, Dad, how many cups, *Dad?* I've had five cups of tea; how many have you had? *Dad! Dad!* . . .'

He slowly put his paper down and said, ever so slowly, in a quiet voice:

'I've *had* . . . sufficient.'

He liked quiet, classical music, and cleaning his shoes ready for work on Monday morning's which drove our mother mad. Later in life he joined the St. John Ambulance Brigade. He had always wanted to be a doctor and that was as close as he was going to get. They threw him out of St. John when he had reached 85 after 25 years' service and I don't think he ever got over it. When he passed away, and I was with my mum early the following morning, she was in tears and said to me,

'Where's *he* gone, Gil?' In her own way, she loved him.

Ever one for a sense of occasion he managed to turn the reading aloud of a simple card into his version of the Saint Crispin's Day speech from *Henry the Fifth*. If Olivier himself had been in that great hall, he would have fallen at my dad's feet in adoration of his rendition.

'*Oh, Thespian!* –'

He began reading from the card:

'I clearly understand (pause) the solemn (extended voice) and binding nature of this Contract (semi-tone lower) and undertake that the Apprentice (extended) will faithfully continue to serve his Master (down a tone) for the full period of the Indenture.

On p-a-i-n (extra extended) of he (pause), he having his throat cut!'

Throat cut! Sorry. Made that last line up. Getting mixed up with the Masons once more.

He ended the reading, turned the card over to address the English bowmen that, in his mind's eye, now stood before him; and seeing the card blank, and with his voice still in full flow not at the end of his oratory, embarrassingly killed it off with a cough, looked up at the top table, smiled, looked at me, then sat down with the ghosts of Shakespeare, St. Cecelia, William Tynedale and the Archbishop Cranmer, looking down at this humble man from their stained-glass windows above: nudged, grinned and generally nodded at each other in agreement at a job well done.

We then all, at the calling of our names, filed up and signed our indentures. The chairman finished off the occasion with a short talk on the virtues of clean living, hard work, and the putting to the back of our minds thoughts of fornication and other such diversions, and to look to the Lord's book for guidance whenever temptation presented itself.

With the ceremony over we all stood humbled with heads lowered vowing to ourselves that from this day forth we would all be good Christian men, before rushing to the bar at the back of the hall for traditional beer, buns, a smoke and to chat-up the girl behind the counter we'd all had our eyes on from the time we first entered Stationers' Hall.

As one of the lads so eloquently described her in her full earshot, 'She looks as if *she* knows which way's up!'

She – for her part – shook her head in disbelief at his comment; seeing him and the rest of this rag-bag bunch of snotty-nosed, underage apprentices with less money in their pockets than Shylock's scullion, trying to chat-her up with the latest lines from a *Carry On* film, got her own back by giving us strong cider instead of the watered down ale we were supposed to be given. In half an hour, we were all as pissed as rats going home with heads thicker than when we came in – and she with her integrity remaining intact.

7 – PRINT SCHOOL

PART of the condition for apprentices to be indentured with APEF was that as they could not provide a thorough education in composing, the college was to make up the short fall.

The original London College of Printing was in Stamford Street, Waterloo. Having outgrown itself, a new college was built at the Elephant & Castle. During this period annexes specialising in different aspects of the trade were dotted around London. As well as Stamford Street there was one at Back Hill; and another, the City Day College along the London Wall at Aldersgate & Barbican. Although not strictly part of the LCP, City Day College was used for subjects, although nothing to do with printing were considered useful to our education.

It now has the highfalutin title of, The London College of Communication, and is a constituent of the University of the Arts London. It specialises in media-related subjects including advertising, animation, film, graphic design, photography, and sound arts, so there!

The day was split into a morning, afternoon, and evening sessions. Yes, it was intensive even by today's standards in apprenticeship education. City Day was for the morning session. Here we were to study cuneiform and ancient writings of the Babylonians and the like (which surprisingly enough I enjoyed), then over to Stamford Street for an afternoon of theory. Finish at 5pm. Hour break then back to the composing room for practical hand composition until 9pm when it was time to leave. What we were taught and took in over those five years would have counted for a degree these days.

It was intense. More especially for me, who studied for his City & Guilds in addition to the yearly pass required in Hand Composition. Every aspect of type arrangement, in all its forms and complexities were shown in theory. We learned to set complex forms, such as railway time-tables and share market listings with their split fractions. These we had to put into practice in the evening. We quickly learned that what an APEF house offered was barely the skin of a rice pudding when it came to a thorough understanding of the art of being a fully rounded compositor. But with what we learned at college, when it came to the pressures of advertising campaigns needed for Monday morning newspapers, with copy and layouts not coming in until Friday night, made us sharp and fast. The employers and the printing union quickly came to realise that the taking on of apprentices into this aspect of the trade, coupled with the London College of Printing, was not a mistake. A new breed of apprentice compositor was emerging that could understand complex layouts from some of the top typographic designers working for the number one advertising agencies in London (and in my opinion counted for the world – I include America); could put them into type arrangement, be proofed, sent for approval, returned, corrected and running on presses for some of the most prestigious national magazines and newspapers across the country. None of which could have been achieved by apprentices serving their time in general printing houses. The trade had turned itself around. This was class work of the highest order recognised as such by the most influential companies in the world. Compositor journeymen in ad-setting were the elite, and their remuneration reflected it. I could earn five times more a week than a compositor from the general trade when I came out of 'my time'. Only newspaper compositors commanded a higher wage, but not from any greater skills.

Typographic design, theory and drawing was part of our curriculum at the London College of Printing and I sucked it up. They provided top graphic designers and typographers from agencies to train us. Some of the trade thought it was over-kill: what did you need to know all that for when you'll mostly be producing winkle bags, letterheads, and raffle tickets. But the LCP persisted under the leadership of the then principal, Ellis Thirkettle, to instill the very best that they could offer. As one of the lecturers said to us, you might only be apprentices; and lowly with it; but you're deserving of the best knowledge that is available – and you never know, it might just grow into something that we can only dream.

There was an ethos at the time – that five years of war had put not only Great Britain, but Europe itself on the back foot – to educate and nurture the youth of this nation in ways that had never been seen before. It was recognised by some far-sighted politicians and leaders that the world was changing, and the youth needed to change with it if this country were to survive. Work was plentiful, and young people, girls as well as boys, were given opportunities and training. Training and apprenticeships, that only today after the longest recession in the world have politicians come to realise that a need to learn from post-war austerities, when it came to a wasting young people lives, had to stop if there was to be any future for the country. Mr. Politician remember your history.

'Finished with the soapbox, son?'

'Yes, dad. Sorry!'

'Carry on, then.'

There was a team of us in that year at the LCP. Bruce, my counterpart from Enfield. A guy called Pither, who could dance like a professional; who would have liked to have gone into the acting profession. Norman, 'I hate print', referring to its theory. Then there was Tony the Mod, from Hackney, who had fought pitch battles at Margate against rockers. He had a Lambretta 175 covered in aerials and headlights and wore the regulation Parka. Then there was Woolly. We had sat the entrance exam together and got on well. We thought that we might work for the same company, but it was not to be, I got stuck with Bruce! (*Sorry mate!*)

What none of us liked college-wise was our morning sessions at the City Day. Although having said that, I did become interested later. Here an academic droned on about different forms of writing with a passion that was never going to settle into the heads of testosterone-fuelled youths. A bit of a plain Jane, she took a lot of stick from us group of sixteen-year-olds, which I am ashamed to say being one, I regret. She got her own back though, she wouldn't let us smoke in her class. That lasted until lunchtime. One hour.

One hour, which gave us just enough time to make it from Aldersgate to Stamford Street on the Tube for the afternoon session. Here the first two hours were taken up with layout and type design from a young designer who had set up on his own. He was one of those that gave up part of their time to teach us. Coming from one of the London art colleges he had studied visual arts going on to design opening sequences for some of the James Bond films. We learnt to hand-draw letters, design, produce book jackets, and draw layouts for compositors to follow. Not as easy as it sounds. It involves a lot of measuring and calculation to produce a block of text with a certain number words in a type face and size to fit where you want it to. These days, with pc's – it's a piece of piss.

Second part of the afternoon involved two hours in a classroom of theory from one Mr. Clench. 'You may smoke if you wish.' Hard to believe, but true. You could smoke pretty well anywhere in the College building those days. This theory involved type composition from all the varieties of hand-composition in the trade. There were complex tables for railway and shipping forms. Set in 5¼pt Times Roman – characters and spaces so small between your thumb and index finger you could snap them – with horizontal and vertical brass rules. Then there were stock and share columns for financial pages of newspapers. These all had their own special sorts (or symbols on a pc) not seen in ad-setting, or anywhere else but financial newspapers. All this theory had to be put into practice later in the evening when we attended our last session of the day in the college's comp room.

Then there was mechanical typesetting. Linotype and Intertype machines were used in newspapers. Monotype were more specialist, generally used in the book trade. The Monotype system came in two parts. The first was the keyboard that produced a perforated spool of paper. This was used to run the caster itself. A wonder of mechanical typesetting the Monotype was a masterpiece. To watch one chundling away is pure fascination. It was one of those machines that you just had to wonder who on earth invented such a thing and put it together.

All the time we scribbled in exercise books – we were keen – thirsty for the knowledge. We had been told that at the end of each year an exam was held, and if you didn't pass you couldn't move on. And on £3.19s.6d. for a first-year apprentice no one fancied being stuck on that wage for a second year. Which was a bit of a lie as apprentices, second-year or otherwise, were paid by their company and had nothing to do with the college. But not being so sure of ourselves, it had the desired effect of keeping our heads down just in case they were right. And Mr. Clench, along with all the other teachers were full of worldly wit and information feeding their subjects – that, *and smoke in class too!*

Five o'clock was our first real break of the day, and Waterloo railway station being a five-minute walk away from Stamford Street that was where we headed. Well, there was a bit of life there. Here they had a soup vending machine that dispensed a passable ox-tail. And I say ox-tail with some reservation. My mum made ox-tail soup. It didn't really taste of that. I couldn't really decide whether it was down to the lack of -tail, or perhaps it was ox-. But the hot water was nice, and when you got to the bottom of the plastic cup, if you broke the top of the lid you could stir up the solid brown mass of gunk that had lodged itself at the bottom that had refused to mix itself in with the water when first dispensed. Whatever it was, it did give me an appreciation of my mum's cooking, so it wasn't an all bad experience. The other thing about Waterloo Station was it always had buskers performing which kept us fairly entertained for the hour. Also, it had the office girls going home; always a bonus. Not that any of us could do much about introducing ourselves to them on our paltry income. Spot the celebrity was also another form of entertainment. These were the days of 'bubble-gum' stars, pictures on fag-cards. And in magazines, such as *Picture Post*, *Tit-Bits*; where their only outlet to the public after appearing in whatever film or rock show on television they appeared made them appreciative of being recognised. They weren't surrounded by minders them days; and they didn't all walk pass their fans as if they were incidental to their success. They would actually smile at you. Well, I suppose smiling might have been too strong a word for the facial expression, it could have been more out of sympathy, we were a rum bunch of sixteen-year-olds after all, scrapping out nourishment from soup cups and smoking rollies was not going to endear ourselves to anyone.

Back to Stamford Street for six o'clock. Here it was three hours of hand-setting and make-up into whatever we had been working on in theory. Some of the work took several weeks to complete such was its complexity. When it was finally finished, a proof was taken, then filed into our exercise books, before (thank you God), the best bit, dissing it back into the cases.

Speaking of God, and I'm not referring to the apprentices' masters, I am speaking of The Master in the Sky. The real God. Anyway, alongside our comp room was another that was being used by nuns. Or rather, novices. Young girls partly attired in their habits – and I'm not being disrespectful – they wore the head covering but only part of the full habit. I don't know where they came from but the head nun in charge was a bit of a dragon, chastising them, not so much for our interest in them as sisters- or brother-in-arms following in the tradition of an ancient craft, but just for looking at us. We tried to call out to them, making the usual remarks that boys are apt to make, but not as far as we might had done had they been regular girls, which of course they were; but you know what I mean – out of habit, so to speak.

Going past on my way home after finishing (I was in my third year), I happened upon one of the novice on her own.

She was clearly in distress by the tears running down her cheeks. She had pied, by the look of it, more than one stick-full of type. Balancing precariously in the galley was a paragraph or two that had gone over, shifted down with every line merged half into the one below it. She was trying to push it back, but it wasn't going anywhere but further into a mess. 'Are you ok?' I asked her as reverently as I could, mindful that the head nun, coming out and clocking me with whatever they used to chastise novices with would catch me. She looked at me and was shaking. There was no one about so I went up to her frame and asked her if I should get someone for her. She told me that the sister had made her stay behind to finish her task. And all because she'd struggled to compose a piece of text from copy that was in Italian; a language she was not familiar.

Nor was I. Who is? Apart from maybe the Pope. I told her that she didn't need to be. In fact, I can set type in any language, whether by hand or on a keyboard. But where she was going wrong at that moment was in trying to recover the pied type. Sometimes you can, mainly you can't. Better to begin again. As for the language barrier, it shouldn't make any difference. Where a lot of beginners go wrong, is by trying to remember the spelling of the word. It will get even worse if you have to compose languages of a Slovakian origin, it's not uncommon to have words fourteen characters in length with accents that look as if they come out of a madhouse. There's a trick, but you need to have a thorough knowledge of the case or be able to type on whatever keyboard be it qwerty (typewriter) or etaoin (Linotype line caster) with confidence. It is also important that if you are hand-setting from a case that you are composing from has been laid correctly to your own specifications. Sometimes, compositors change boxes putting letters in another especially if their work is of a specialist nature. Whenever I had a large 'take' that required accuracy and concentration, like a foreign language, I would empty the case of the type, clean it out, then relay it. Only that way could I set without looking at what was being put in my stick instead concentrate on the copy. Once done, it's back to the trick.

Follow copy out the window, is an oft times used quotation, and if accuracy is to be maintained, it's the only way. Being an LCP laid case of type I could take it as read that it would have been laid accurately. Nevertheless, I did a quick check on some of the boxes. They seemed okay. I then took up the nervous novice's stick from her and ushered her to one side. She looked anxious for the pair of us, fearing the sister returning, but I went ahead anyway.

I took up her copy that she had laying across the case – another bad habit. Placing it in the copy-holder above the angle of the case at eye height I began setting. The first paragraph was in English. An Unction for administering to the sick or dying. Not the most cheerful of copy. Then the Latin began. I looked at the copy and studied it character at a time, moving smoothly around the case, setting line after line. In less than five minutes I had a stick-full. Putting it on the galley, I placed a lead clump against it to keep it secure, then carried on. Time might be against me; I wasn't going to take any chances on pieing this lot. Another five minutes and the Unction was finished. As nice a piece of Italian composition as you'll see anywhere inside the Vatican, if I said so myself. I quickly tied it up.

'It's done, now go and proof it. I've got a home to go to.'

She smiled. 'What if the sister asks me how I did it?'

This sister of hers clearly didn't expect her to complete her task but was punishing her for whatever sin she thought she had committed. 'You've heard of a white lie?' She hesitantly nodded. 'Well, tell her you had Divine inspiration. She won't be able to argue with that.'

PRINT SCHOOL

Our day was normally finished by 9 pm, except this evening, when it went to 9.45 pm. I ran down to Waterloo, got the Tube and was back in Tooting by 10.45 pm. Supper, then to bed, exhausted.

Thank God, I'm back to work in the morning.

8 – TROTS AND TROTTING

THE WORD *Trots*, apart from being slang for diarrhoea, has another altogether different connotation in the compositors' world. Although, having said that, and thinking about it, the medical definition has been used on more than one occasion as an excuse for a following day off work, usually a Monday, usually after a recovery from the over indulgence of a Saturday night's session of ten pints of brown and mild before retiring to the Taj for an oriental supper. If you did discount dysentery for Trots, there are two other definitions. The first is a shortened version of Trotting, meaning to lead someone up the garden path, as in the verb transitive: exaggerate, e.g. 'I had 14 pints of brown and mild and two vindaloos on Saturday night.'

First journeyman. 'You're *Trotting*!'

Second journeyman. 'Only a little, it was 10 pints actually.'

On reflection, not a very good example as it could still be misconstrued as, 'I've got a touch of the *Trots* after floating a plate of Ghandi's revenge on a stomach full of beer at the weekend.'

A-a-a-a. I'll move on, shall I?

The third definition: a practical joke. And comp rooms were full of them. From cutting the article on page 3 from page 1 with the, *continued on page 3,* out of a companion's newspaper after he's read page 1. Especially funny if it's a résumé of Saturday's match at Leyton Orient or Tottenham. They had wonderful support as many of the journeymen I worked with came from north London. Apprentices got a lot of mileage out of that one, usually because they'd bought the papers in and got to doctoring them before passing them over.

Then there's the old-time favourite of putting toy caps around rollers of the presses before the unsuspecting pressman switches it on and moves it off. Roars of laughter and heart-attacks all round from the rattle of what sounds like machine-gun fire. Then there's creeping up behind a journeyman and knotting up his apron strings – tight – watching them when 'lining-off' trying to extricate themselves into a position where they could untie it. Or. The all-time classic. The strategic placing of paper spurs on the back of a journeyman's shoes, especially after they've been worked on with bright coloured stars cut and shaped. As the poor soul strides off up Earlham Street to the underground station after a day's work and still not having noticed, with us apprentices hanging out of the windows, holding our sides to stop the pain from laughing.

Another great one, from a journeyman's point of view. You only get caught on this one the once. As I said before, an ad-setting firm needed to carry an awful lot of cases of type to function. Apart from the cases that are stored in the frames where the composing is carried out, there was also what were known as tall-boys. Not unlike a large wardrobe, they carried cases in them to the point where you could just about reach up to the top one with arms outstretched, easing it gently out, taking hold of its edge and with the flat of the palm of your hand, balance it in mid-air before bringing it to shoulder height for transit. As I have also mentioned a fully loaded case can go to 30kg in weight, and a lot of our tall-boys were a couple of flights of stairs up and round corners away from the comp room.

I was assisting a journeyman that was bit of a bully-boy if he could get away with it. We were at the stone, and he had just pulled out a forme that needed correcting. Sliding it from the forme rack he carried it in both hands against his stomach before lifting it up and dropping it flat onto the stone with a bang. It was a full-page broadsheet ad in size, and as formes go it was heavy, and was about to be made even heavier with the replacement of the wooden furniture surrounding the text with clumps of lead to prevent the foundry press from flattening it. The type that was used for its title was 84pt Venus Extra Bold Extended. A solid and meaty face with an even meatier case holding it.

'Fetch me the case, it's in the top store, would you?'

I dutifully obliged. Fortunately, 84pt was quite low to the bottom of the tall-boy, nevertheless, it still had to be brought up to my shoulder height and wasn't light. I negotiated it down the two flights and into the comp room mindful that if I had a tumble with it, I could have a nasty accident. Still, if it was wanted.

Going to the journeyman's frame I lifted it onto the slant and went over to him and told him it was there. He then carried out the corrections, replacing battered type, battered rules and minor corrections to the text which happened to be in 8pt Plantin. After ten minutes or so, he asked me to get him a lower case w from the case that I had brought down. I selected it and

TROTS AND TROTTING

handed it to him, another ten minutes and he was starting to lock the forme up again, planing it as he was going.

'You can take it back now, I'm finished.'

I was never sure if he pulled that one on me out of a sense of trotting, or because he had a mean streak in him. I suspected the latter.

Not all revenge is a dish best served cold. Setting fire to a journeyman's paper while he's reading it had always been good for a laugh. A lighted match brought slowly to the bottom of the page before a quick exit out the door. If he were a bit slow witted; engrossed in the sports page the flames would catch him good. As far as Trots go this one could be a tad on the dangerous side.

Speaking of fires, I am reminded of when the Great Fire of Chicago took place. A reporter for the then *Chicago Republican*, one Michael Ahern, came out with the Trot of all time when he reported that the fire was started by a cow belonging to Patrick and Catherine O'Leary when it kicked over a lighted lantern in its barn. Mr. Ahern, obviously not to be outdone by the Great Fire of London in 1666 being started at Thomas Farriner's bake house in Pudding Lane, felt a need to go one better. Unfortunately, he had to rescind his story in 1896 as little more than colourful copy. The *Chicago Republican*, faring little better than the reportage of the start of the Great Fire of London in the *London Gazette*, Ahern's apology was its last by-line before it too burned down in the Chicago fire.

However, I digress – *Trots*. All the time these go on, there's George Good, overseer, and one, that if there ever was one, that should know better for allowing this anti-social behaviour, roaring with laughter, barking out his familiar iterative of, 'Aha! aha! aha! Howya! howya! howya! typical apps. What would you do with them?' All very well until he's on the wrong end of one. That was when Bruce and I inadvertently took him down when we trotted him good and proper, and all quite by chance, we never meant to. These days you would lose your job for such pranks. And we did come close, or so he said. For we took him at his word at the time.

Started innocently enough. Bruce had a look at one of my layouts for a job I was about to begin when I was out mumping. Clocked a couple of type sizes and faces that were obscure and unlikely to be used by anyone else that day and deposited a large dollop of black ink inside the handle of one of the cases. Naturally, I got round to getting the case, shoving my fingers inside the handle disappearing them up into the ink. Sniggers of laughter from all concerned. I looked up at him, immediately guessing the source of the trot. Seeing him and the look on his face I nod and smile, the smile that he knows that I know his laughter is going to be short-lived. Putting it to the back of my mind for a while, I pull out the other case getting caught for the second time. What is known in the trade as a double-trot. With that kind of trot, you're going to have to leave it sometime before following up with something similar, unless something else comes immediately to mind. It didn't, and George (with hearty laughter), suggested that I forget it and clean the case handles up, which I did, but being an app, forget-it is not part of our vocabulary. More . . . to get even.

The trouble was it got slightly out of hand. I caught Bruce on the first case, that was not difficult, but not on a subsequent one. Getting desperate I applied the black stuff to several others he was likely to use that day. At the same time, Bruce was now doing the same to me. Before we knew it, there was something like thirty cases scattered around the comp room racks and frames that had been got at. Now the journeymen were getting caught and the joke was beginning to wear thin. All the time, George, was still laughing. Then he got caught, with knobs on. Wearing one of his tonic mohair's, he hadn't at first noticed that he was spreading black ink down his jacket pocket while retrieving his packet of cigarettes. Then somehow, down his face, half up the lighted cigarette hanging, smoking from his lips he took the expression of a *Black and White Minstrel* half done (a popular television programme the *Minstrels* ran from 1958 until being axed in its white man blacked-up face format in 1975 as no longer being acceptable). He hadn't realised until it was pointed out to him by the deputy overseer, Fred Howe, what he looked like. When the laughter stopped, he looked at the pair of us before disappearing into the washroom with a tin of carbon tetrachloride and a rag, only to emerge ten minutes later looking worse than when he went in. He now had the addition of patches of diluted ink and chemical cleaner down the suit. His face rouged up from a reaction to the chemical cleaner. All in all, he looked a right mess. Apart from anything else, this was his second tonic mohair since the last one had half the pocket ripped off. He looked at the pair of us, pointed his finger and flick waved it at us to follow him to his frame. Now it's worth mentioning here that George's desk and frame was at the end of the comp room stationed to give him a commanding view of the comp room to keep an eye on proceedings, so to speak. From here he could hand out disciplines in the form known universally as verbal bollickings to journeymen that were to get the edge of his tongue if they were out of order. Not a vindictive man, and still with his sense of humour for what was likely to occur when administering these, bollickings, he would invariably stand in the position so that his back would be to the comp room, leaving room for yet another trot, and one of his own favourites: that of the poor soul having to restrain himself from laughing while being dressed-down with an audience. Seeing what was going to take place, the word would soon go around. Here the companionship would lower themselves behind their frames giving the impression that the comp room was empty. With the intention of popping their heads up from various frames and corners in a haphazard fashion; placing their thumbs on their noses and wiggling their fingers at you before going back down again. Anyone that has suffered such torture while at the same time being reprimanded will know just how painful this can be. The juxtaposition of the emotions humility and laughter send the brain's thought processes into a free-fall that is difficult to control, and which is only going to end one way. And George knew it.

So, there we were, Bruce and me. George with his back to the comp room he begins. He goes on to talk of the historical needs to balance work and fun; of the need to keep them separate and in their place; of propriety and the respect for one's fellow worker and to know when one's taking things too far; that property – with the emphasis on suits – being not cheap only obtained by the sweat of one's labours are easily lost, as in his suit, hand-made in Golder's Green by a Jewish Russian émigré that had escaped one of Stalin's pogrom's.

He went on. When he did so, all his worldly-wise wisdoms came to the fore, none of it relevant to the matter in hand. But we were a captive audience and so we suffered, heads lowered until . . .

We are suddenly aware that the comp room is empty and that something is about to happen. And it does. Up pops the gesticulating face of little Jimmy, thumb to his nose, behind his frame and as quickly lowers out of sight, only to emerge from behind another several yards away from the first. We are finished in the expectation of another. There is nowhere to go. Grinning and smiling faces are everywhere, popping up like automatons at a seaside pier slot machine show. We break out in, at first, mock laughter heavily disguised as coughing and sneezing, but which doesn't fool George.

'Do you find this a laughing matter?'

He is looking at me. For myself, I correct the emotion and become stony-faced. He then looks to Bruce, who is going through a similar roller coaster of the tremors. George then looks back at me, and I am going again. Holding my breath, biting my tongue, trying to control the pressure of a snot build up from my nose, I reach for my handkerchief to bury my face into it before farting.

'Well!' George bellows. 'I am waiting for an answer.'

George knows exactly what's going on. He's not the overseer for nothing and determined to get as much mileage out of our discomfort as he can. 'It's them!' I finally manage to blurt out. 'They're making me laugh.' He turns around. Everyone in the comp room is now standing at their frames working away like beavers, straight-faced, giving an impression of industrial sobriety. He turns back to me. I fart once more.

'Making you laugh. Who's making you laugh?' I don't reply. I feel a fool. 'Right, I want every bit of ink removed from those cases. I want it done now, and I want it done properly. *And!*' He lowers his voice pitch and pace, 'If this ever happens again, to me, or anyone else.' He points his finger in the direction of the managing director's office. 'You'll be up them stairs so fast, your feet won't touch the ground. Do I make myself clear?' We nod, relieved that this is finally over. 'Get out of my sight and get this mess cleaned up. I don't want to hear another word from the pair of you for the rest of the day.'

We both reply, 'Yes, George.'

We walk up the comp room whispering. Bruce says, trying to contain his laughter, 'Did you see the state of his suit—?'

I'm in fits, '*Fucking 'ell*. Yeh. Hope you can remember where you put the rest of that ink, 'cause I can't.'

Two weeks later. It's Monday morning. George steps out of the lift and into the comp room. Closing the lift doors behind him, shouts, '*Goody good*, gents.' Wearing a newly tailored suit (the other, obviously beyond redemption), he has opted for yet another tonic mohair (the Jewish–Russian émigré has just booked another holiday), then with the bearing of the Duke of

Kent, marches down the comp room at a pace, this time catching the pocket on a pack of brass strip rule that is protruding from its rack, takes the seam open to just below the arm pit.

Now in this life some occasions/events will make you laugh, and some will make you – not laugh. And laughter, being an emotional expression that no two people might have a sense of at the same time, when it comes to a crowd, like, say an audience, a comedian will make a joke, a clown a prat-fall, there is, generally speaking, and regardless of one person's sense of humour over another's, the spontaneity of the herd instinct of not wanting to be the odd one out, that might be thought of as not getting the joke.

Psychologically, there is a name for this strange phenomenon: it borders on mass hysteria, and every comedian worth his salt knows of it, hence when he's on a roll the first laugh heard feeds on itself and infects the audience. All the comedian has to do now is keep the one-liners coming. Nobody can be exactly sure why, but just occasionally this doesn't happen. In the case of George and his new suit, this was just one of those times and I put it down to discretion being the better part of valour, no court jester was going to risk his neck on the block to humour this king. Not this time.

9 – TICKETS PLEASE!

THE NORTHERN LINE on Transport for London's map starts at Morden and extends to Mill Hill East. At the time of writing it is 36 miles long and has 50 stations. It has fingers of other lines coming off it at tangents. The whole network covers some 520 square miles of London from the edge of Surrey in the south to Middlesex in the north; and from Middlesex in the west to Kent in the east; making it the world's largest urban railway network. It is still growing.

Cockney rhyming slang for the Tube is Oxo, as in Oxo cube – Tube. Its logo includes a roundel and incorporates the type face known as Johnston after the designer Edward who devised it in 1916.

Current operator is London Underground Limited, a wholly owned subsidiary of Transport for London.

All this maze of tunnels and bolt holes that appear above ground as station entrances are the quickest way in and around London if you discount two wheels. The two wheels that were available to me when I started work only lasted as long as Keith lived down the road from me. When he eventually moved to Ewell in Surrey it was left for me to make my own way into London; this meant the Tube. Which also meant money having to be shelled out by way of fares. I was not impressed. The pittance of a wages of just £3.19s 6d a week was hardly a sum to encourage honesty. So, having reasoned that the train that I needed to get me to work was going that way anyway I did not see that 'not paying' was in any way taking pecuniary advantage (Well, I did, but that was my justification). A fail proof scheme for avoiding this penal charge was needed.

Now in those days there was not always a ticket inspector checking to make sure that you had a ticket when you got on the train. This meant it was possible to board without such a paid for chit. The problem came when you arrived at your destination. Here the ticket collector needed to have your ticket as proof that you had not only paid the fare, but that it was also the amount from the station in question to the station of destination. If you did not have one the only two things that you could say (assuming you didn't own up to fiddling), were that you must have lost it or that you came from Tooting Broadway and that you were late for work not having the time to queue up for the purchase of said ticket. At this point he would collect the money from you. Or, that you came from a station that was only, say two stops away, and pay the fare from there. A not inconsiderable saving. Before you did that though you had to make sure that the station you had elected did not have a ticket inspector on duty when you supposedly went through. The man taking your ticket from you at your destination would know that because they would have told him that there was an inspector on so-and-so station and at what time. So, the answer to that one was to get off at the stop that you would be electing as your place of departure, go up the escalators and see for yourself. If there was no inspector re-board the following train to your destination, then with confidence as you go through, pennies in hand say, 'Waterloo, please!'

'Three pence!' the inspector would growl smelling a rat, not quite being able to feel the fur on its back.

If there happened to be an inspector at Waterloo, then the only thing that you could do was to get back on the train and when you arrived at your destination, own up to having travelled from Tooting Broadway.

'No, you don't, I recognise you, and you live at Waterloo?'

'Sleeping at me girlfriends, wasn't I,' I would reply cockily, walking away whistling, feeling the thought of cheeky little bleeder coming from him into the back of my neck. I had to pay the full fare on those occasions, but you can't win them all.

The fare from Tooting Broadway to Leicester Square was 1/6d return, if I could get away with 6d a day that would save me half a crown a week. After my wages had had the hammering of a weekend, and paying me mum, I only had about ten bob in my pocket, so this was quite a saving. Unfortunately, this was not to last.

'*Oi! Charlie!*' The full force of the attention to commandment hit me in the back of my neck before I had gone five yards. The inspector seeing me had turned his thought into something more proactive than what I had imagined. I turned round to see him waving his finger back and forth in my direction in the indication that he hadn't finished with me, yet. I walked back. 'Now, sonny, or whatever your name is, us inspectors on the London Underground take a pretty dim view of those that evade their fare.' He took on the attitude of a man about to present a sermon – not for the first time! 'We inspectors on the London Underground take our jobs seriously, and contrary to what you might think, or have heard, we know exactly what is going on and where. The grapevine that is the inspectors of the London Underground are like monks, we are a closed, silent order, going about our work diligently priding ourselves on our results.' He looked me full in the face and issued his ultimatum. 'Get caught again trying to evade your fare and you'll be dragged up before the courts to answer to the charge of taking pecuniary advantage. Such advantages are taken a dim view of by the Beaks of this land and likely to find you with a fine that will make your fare seem a pittance in comparison.' He smiled. 'Be here tomorrow, and every day, with your one and sixpenny ticket in your hand, and we'll say no more about your past . . . misdemeanours. Do I make myself clear?'

I nodded.

'Good. 1/6d it is then. Print it on your very soul.'

So, that was going to be that, the end of my free rides. But there were over ways of augmenting my income.

10 – SOHO

ONE lunch time I happened along Old Compton Street in Soho when an old bookshop in one of its off alleys caught my eye. Looking in its window I sensed someone standing next to me – a bit close. What one might refer to these days as, *Being in yer face*.

It was a woman, I guessed to be in her seventies, dripping in make-up and wearing, what I could only describe as clothes from *Mother Goose*. She had open-toed sandals that sported nicotine stained, chipped, with red varnished toenails protruding from them. Almost inaudibly she muttered something to me reminiscent of the words: 'Could you direct me to the Bank?'

I turned to her. 'Sorry, what did you say?'

Still muffling, she repeated herself.

Her voice playing out in my head as I tried to make sense of her words again, then I cottoned on, or thought I did: '*The Bank!* Oh, yeh. You know Tottenham Court Road? Take the Central line from there. I think – three or four stops—'

She looked at me, then smiling sweetly said, 'No honey, I said, "*would you like a wank?*"'

I froze.

She smiled and indicated where she would take me.

'Only five bob, down the end of that alley behind those boxes.' I looked into the newspaper and general rubbish infested alleyway with the boxes she indicated. One was printed, Fish Fingers, another Pineapple Chunks, and yet another, Gherkins in Saline from Athens. I panicked. Turning on my heels I started to run. Looking back, I shouted, 'I've only got 1/6d, and I need that for my train fare—'

A heard her voice in the distance shouting back at me, something on the lines of, '*That'll do nicely, luvvy . . .*'

What is known as the square mile is bounded by streets on four sides. Oxford Street, Regent Street, Leicester Square, and the Charing Cross Road; and all but a short walk from CVC in Earlham Street to Soho.

Soho, an area of London popular with tourists and that which you are advised to treat with respect if you are to stay out of trouble is cosmopolitan, colourful, artistic and musical. It was notoriously dangerous then and remains so today. With drug-dealing, prostitution, and strip-joints it's all too easy to find yourself in the middle of something you've no business. People can wind up dead for stepping out of line; fortunately, they are mostly of the criminal persuasion. A day-time visitor is likely to go round unmolested, which is when I had occasion to be there. I got to know a lot of people while mumping type; they for their part got to know me, and I was treated for what I was, someone making a living in the area. An apprentice that worked and had every right to be there. We were mostly left alone not heckled and encouraged into the brothels and strip joints that lined the greater parts of it as visitors were. The working girls that frequented public houses the like of the

Helvetia – a drinking hole we used occasionally – knew one or two of the journeymen I worked with, so even they got to know me, and that was as far as it went. Printing apprentices were out-of-bounds when it came to being ripped off or robbed. CVC was not the only ad-setting house in the area; and we were all given that same respect.

If you had a night off however, and went there, then all bets were off. One Christmas, all us apprentices from the ad-setters in the square mile went on a pub-crawl – about ten of us. During the course of the evening someone suggested it would be a good idea to go to a strip joint. It wasn't me, honest, gov'nor. An experience tame by today's standards, but nevertheless . . .

A bouncer wearing an evening suit, with black slick-backed and Brylcremed hair stood at the top of the stairs beckoned us down. A basement dive in St. Anne's Court, called, *Gigi's*, with pictures of scantily-clad girls lining its peeling pink painted walls. 'Only ten bob boys, half a nicker, come on, show's just starting.'

We looked at each other. One nodded and smiled. 'Come on then boys, hardly going to break the bank, it'll be a laugh.'

We all agreed with him and dug into our pockets and gave the bouncer our ten bob notes and disappeared down the stairs in eager anticipation. Then we came to another door, with another bouncer. 'Hello boys,' he said, 'coming in – ten bob.'

'Yeh, we've already paid, the guy up the steps.' He looked at me then went up three steps. There was no one there. 'Come on, half a nicker, or *fuck-off!*'

Easy isn't it. As quick as that. You just know you've been taken and there's nothing you can do about it. One of the lads said, 'What'll we do now?'

'Pay another ten bob, and hope there's no more doors,' I replied with a shrug of, *We've been stuffed we might as well go the rest of the way.*

He took our money and we all piled in.

Dingy was not the word for the – and I use the term loosely – auditorium that confronted us, and in retrospect that wasn't really a very good word for it either. As our eyes adjusted to the seediness of the dark, it just didn't get any better. Someone shouted, 'Oi! You lot, sit the *fuck* down, you're blocking the fanny view.'

With comments like that you just know you're in for an evening of high sophistication and culture, don't you?

We did as we were bade. We shuffled along the seats that looked as if they'd come out of a cinema that had taken a direct hit from a German night-time *Blitzkrieg* during WWII and sat down. I couldn't help noticing that the three front rows were full of men with overcoats over their laps. You'd have thought they'd left them in the cloakroom, might have been more comfortable . . . still . . . each to his own. *And* the place didn't smell too good either. Sort of a cross between body odour, cheap aftershave, fags, and wet dog *and* something else scarcely mentionable in case it was. We all looked at each other and sort of smiled and sniffed. Then a stage light came on and the curtains opened, and there they were, what we paid a quid each for. Five girls – there's that loose term again – dressed as

Roman Goddesses. Now we're all familiar with the Fall of the Roman Empire: its debaucheries and general degeneration; but this was pushing the boat out a bit too far for even that, they were . . . 'kin' 'orrible as Goddesses go. Standing there with urns on their shoulders, draped in what should have been silks but looking more like bedsheets and surplus army blankets. There was a small upright table between them with an ashtray and two smoking cigarettes with a glass (I guessed to be gin and tonic). We just sat there astounded. Not the three rows in front though, with their overcoats over their laps working overtime, they were giving it what for, excitedly shouting encouragements the like of, 'Get 'em off!' 'Where'd you keep your lunch, love?', and other such terms of endearment. But all credit to them, those Goddesses stood their ground.

During the 'Sixties, strip tease performers were not allowed to move. More a pageant framed in still-life. It didn't stop the first three rows of rolling eyes though, they just carried on, 'Go on, move yourselves!'

One girl did. Putting down her urn, she leaned forward, then picking up a cigarette from the ashtray, took a drag, put it back, went to her G&T, took a sip, then finally turning to the other girls shouted out, 'Must be the *fucking* school holidays!'

That was when the curtain came down, followed closely by a police raid.

Now I'm not one to cast assertions, but, if you have a police raid ten minutes after the start of every show, and they allow you to re-open if you promise in future to act as proper and responsible proprietors, you can take a lot of ten bobs in an evening. Welcome to the seedier side of life, you deserve what you get. And that includes the Metropolitan Police, or people dressed as them.

11 – A WET LUNCH

THERE are of course more educational establishments to while away an hour's lunch in London than Soho. The call 'Line-off' by the Father of the Chapel (Black Pat) signals an exodus of men and apprentices to whatever they have planned. Some shop, some go to the museums and art galleries and some pub it.

Earlham Street is on the edge of Covent Garden Market. Cambridge Circus is to one side while Soho is to the other. Since moved and relocated to Hatfields on the South of the River Thames because of traffic congestion, the old Covent Garden is now a tourist attraction. Full of wine bars, buskers, lively music venues, and even a genuine Cornish pasty shop. But not then. Then, it was a full working market supplying vegetables to the entire country. Much of its traffic doubled up by having the dual role of selling by growers and buying by wholesalers.

Market business began in the early hours after midnight, and by lunch-time most was over; but to wander round was still interesting.

Inside the workings of the market there is the site of the first Punch and Judy show to be exhibited in England. Brought to this country by its Italian creator Pietro Gimonde it made its first appearance in England May 9, 1662. Described by one of the watching audience, Samuel Pepys in his diary as '. . . an

Italian puppet play, that is within the rails there, which is very pretty.' Close to the site is the Covent Garden Opera House. A grand building among the unlikely setting of smell and noise and general untidiness of the market; but not without contrast. Bow Street and its equally famous police station is also now a famous attraction. (I had business there on one occasion. More later.) And there are innumerable public houses: the Opera Tavern, the Nags Head, to mention but a few, all still in existence. As for Earlham Street itself, heading upwards toward Cambridge Circus, the street was lined with stalls and cafes run by Greeks, Cypriots, Turkish, and Italians. The Italians famous for their ice-cream and pizza pies; the Greeks for their shish kebabs wrapped in pitta bread gave the street an ambience akin to Asia Minor. This was colour in all its shades. You could buy any food you fancied, and the smells were unbelievable as you walked along. These were delicatessens in the raw before they became fashionable. The Greeks arrived in Soho before the Italians by about 200 years, shortly after the Greek Orthodox Church's persecution by the Ottoman Empire. Here they built their own church free from such persecution. London was a welcoming secular city and Soho's Greek Street was named in their honour. The Italians came in the 19th century from a poverty-torn country. Imprisoned during the Second World War as enemy aliens they were eventually accepted by the British people. A second wave came in the fifties when we had labour shortages. Our country would have been all the poorer without this invasion of aliens.

The local pub for CVC was the *Nags Head*, and it was there

that I first discovered John Courage. God, he was strong. *The Opera Tavern* was another haunt that we frequented. You'd get a lot of actors in there that were working the matinee shifts at the theatres that abounded St. Martin's Lane and Cambridge Circus. When out of my time I visited it and being a member of the British Sub-Aqua Club, No 2 Branch, I recognised and introduced myself to a known member of the BS-AC No 1 Branch and a fellow diver. A tall blonde-haired chap who was making his mark entertainment wise. Jon Pertwee, later to be known as *Dr. Who*, *Wurzel Gummidge* and *Nunkey*, a character from the radio show, *The Navy Lark*, was not a man you would have expected to have achieved the level of a First Class diver. But then later discovering that he worked for Naval intelligence alongside Ian Fleming reporting directly to Winston Churchill that wouldn't have been any great surprise had I known then. He sported desert boots, corduroy trouser and purple shirt complete with cravat. Ostentatious dressing was just coming into vogue then. 'Good to have met you,' he said on parting, 'what did you say your name was?'

'Gil,' I replied.

'See you all at sea sometime, young man.' He shook me by the hand and was gone. I never saw him again in the flesh.

He died in his sleep in New York in 1996. At his funeral in Putney Vale; and at his request, he was cremated with a toy Worzel Gummidge, the scarecrow character he portrayed in the children's television series created by Barbara Euphan Todd from the books of the same name.

Of course, a lot of the west end public houses attracted

celebrities that weren't retired, merely resting between jobs. Their conversations loud and articulate, drinking themselves stupid, not realising that their acting days were over. Media intrusion was more concerned with those proactive in their profession; technology was not as fast as today. They could afford to be noticed without being *noticed*. A dead give-away was the wearing of dark glasses.

Two or three of the pubs in the market, like other markets, had different opening times from the usual to accommodate the unusual working routines of market traders and porters. There they could get a pint and a bacon sandwich any time after midnight up to 7 am. Strictly speaking they were for market people, but they unofficially catered for others. Print workers who had been on the night shift at *The Daily Herald*, Bow Street police station, and of course ad-setting journeymen. Although once inside everyone worked for the market, and with the Bow Street Runners in attendance who was going to ask what anyone did in the market. During those early hourly sessions there would be twice as many people working for the market than were employed.

One of my favourite lunch-time watering holes was the Irish house known as *Mooney's* on Cambridge Circus. Here you could get the best drop of draught Guinness outside of Ireland (I've been to Dublin, drunk it, and you could). The barman would put your glass under the pump and pull and pull again. Then taking a knife he would skim the head off and pull again. It had a top like driven snow. He would then pitch a cloverleaf design on it with another pull.

'I asked for a pint, not a shave,' I once cheekily said to the barman in my younger day. He gave me an old-fashioned look, took the beer away from me saying, 'When yer old enuf to shave, sonny, yer'll be old enuf to enjoy this, now close the door on yer way out.'

I watched my manners after that.

An accompaniment to the Guinness was the bar lunch of Irish sausages, beans and mash; two pints of the Black Velvet to wash it down: total price 8/- (40p). Try and get back across Cambridge Circus and set some type with that lot inside you.

Now, although in the five years as an apprentice; and having drunk in possibly every pub in the square mile in that time, I don't want anyone to think that's all I did. All the places of interest that tourists come to see in London were always in striking distance of a lunch-time walk. In those five years I can honestly say that I never ever got bored.

When I first ventured out for a lunch-time stroll, making my way to the top of Earlham Street and into Seven Dials on that first day, I was close to being overwhelmed that I was working as an apprentice in the greatest city in the world. London was under my feet. I turned left into St. Martin's Lane and the St. Martin's Theatre where Agatha Christie's play The Mousetrap was only in its ninth year. Although premiered at the Theatre Royal in Nottingham in 1952, at the time of writing, its 64th year, it has been at the St. Martin's ever since.

Turning left I came into the Strand happening upon a government surplus store. I looked in the window, it was an

A WET LUNCH

Aladdin's cave in there. Cameras, binoculars, rucksacks, tents, sleeping bags, boots. *Boots!* Hanging up in a great heap, what were known as mosquito boots. Suede. Leather bottoms. Ex-US Marine surplus from the Vietnam War. Just what I could do with when I go camping and at five bob a pair – *bargain!* I'll be back on Friday when I get paid. I walked on.

People were everywhere; and what traffic. Rolls Royce's, sports cars of various descriptions, every other vehicle seemed to be either a taxi or a bus. And everyone seemed to be in a hurry. Absolute chaos. I needed to cross.

I started by waiting for a convenient gap in the traffic. That was a mistake for a start. There are no gaps in London traffic. I then thought I would try and dive between two vehicles and hope that they would slow down enough for me to get across that way. No way. They just sped up and tried to run me down. Back on the pavement I thought again.

Then I saw something. A bowler hated gentleman, pin-striped suit, blue-striped shirt, white fly-winged collar. Carrying a briefcase, he had it off to a T. A veritable master of the Queen's highway on legs. A human being that had somehow managed to survive in this alien environment. It looked easy. Well, he made it so.

He walked along the pavement in a casual manner, then when the traffic wasn't looking, he increased his pace. Slowly at first, then getting faster until he was going at roughly the same speed as the traffic was. A quick glance to his right, and then he was out in the road. Running alongside a car that was passing him, then increasing his speed he overtook it, slowing down slightly as he slipped into the second lane of traffic. They, the second lane, having seen what he was doing speeded up. He let them go, but they were not looking what they were doing and were now closing-up too fast to the cars in front of them, braking hard. Then before the third car could accelerate away our man was between them and in the middle of the road. No-man's land where he could gather his wits.

Having assessed the new situation, he changed direction to consider the flow of traffic going the other way and repeated the process before landing safely on the other side. All he had to do now was slow his pace to a walk, reinvent his dignity, cough, shake his head and resume his business direction.

Bloody fantastic that, I thought to myself, I'll give that a try. Now I've done some hairy things in my short life. Diving off Chertsey bridge in Surrey into the Thames. Canoeing over weirs with lockkeepers screaming at me to stop. Rock climbing, and generally making people wonder what I was going to get up to next, especially me mum, but this, crossing the road was a real challenge. It had to be done.

I started out all right, got to no-man's land, then it all went wrong. I stepped off the middle island went to go in front of a car and changed my mind at the same time as the car I was about to run in front of braked to stop hitting me. Still running on a changed direction, I managed to hook my leg on his bumper. Breaking free on one leg I hobbled right into the path of a chap on a push-bike and nearly had the pair of us over.

'What the bleedin' 'ell you up to you great stupid ****. A car's horn blotted out the rest of what he was saying to me

A WET LUNCH

(probably some good advice regarding my probability of finishing my apprenticeship if I don't jolly well buck up my ideas and watch out where I'm going); but the fight for survival had already reached the point of no return. I fended the next car off with my hand having changed my direction and with a final skip and a jump landed on the pavement on the other side of the road falling against a shop window.

People were now staring first at me. The following traffic hearing car horns and shouting, not knowing why joined in the cacophony. I shrugged and carried on up the Strand as if nothing had happened. My heart was pounding.

Now finding myself outside the Savoy hotel I was reminded of my dad, who had once had a job there as a page-boy. He must have been as half-brained as me. He had managed to get the sack from this illustrious establishment for falling down the stairs with a tray full of glasses after taking two at a time. Funny thing about my old dad. He was a socialist taken with the rich and famous. Because of their wealth he would extol what they could do as opposed to what he could not. Of how they dressed. He told me about the Savoy Tailors' guild, the bespoke gentlemen's outfitters for kings and the well-to-do. And here they were. I stared in the window. From the inside looking out I must have looked like some dress-poor Dickensian urchin seeing clothes for the first time. They had suits in there at over £200. My dad had just bought a suit for me in Streatham. They were the Jackson family tailors, George Lyle and he'd bought all his suits from there, nearly three of them. Keith, my brother, also had his suits made there. My suit had cost the princely sum of £15. You could imagine what these suits were like at the Savoy compared with mine. Although, to be fair to George Lyle, he was still a bespoke tailor and most importantly, Jewish. The cut was no better than mine though, it was the cloth that separated them. For nobody can cut and stitch like a Jewish tailor, and George was up there with the best. Perhaps he had at one time been apprenticed there before setting up on his own.

They also had hand-made leather shoes for sale. You could expect to pay around £30 for them then; I was determined that I would get myself a decent pair of them when I had got enough money up.

The front entrance to the Savoy hotel is impressive. No parking problems there for residents, you just turn in, or should I say, sweep in. Cars turn, limousines sweep. Here top-hatted doormen open the passenger door to release jewel-splatted personages accompanied by overfed gentleman. A high-voiced lady of impeccable Cheltenham Lady's College tones says, 'Tell my chauffeur to pick me up at four,' while at the same time pushing a half-crown into the man's hand.

'Very good, madam,' he replies in a half-cough manner his hand to his mouth and head bowed in time-honoured fashion.

When the 'royal' personages are clear, he walks around the limo to the Lady's driver, 'Oi! You, *laddie!*'

The chauffeur reading his copy of the *Racing Post* looks up and takes immediate umbrage at this intrusion into his business of a second-hand nature from someone below his station, 'Who you calling, *laddie?*' says he at the same time climbing out of the limousine and taking the doorman by the scruff of the throat pinning him to the glass-fronted Hoté d'Cuisine display board at a height somewhere between the Braised Livers and Bacon, immediately above the Woodcock with Pear. 'I'll fix your face for you, *laddie!* m'lad, speaking to me like that!'

The doorman squeaks out from behind an ever tightening collar stud, 'I only said four o'clock.'

The chauffeur releases him. 'See to your own duty, I heard m'lady, I'm not deaf,' says he. He then climbs back into his limousine continuing to read the form for Right Tack running in the 2000 Guineas at Newmarket that day.

The doorman readjusting his dress and feeling brave as the chauffeur putting his paper away starts the engine and pulls off.

'There's no need to take that attitude with me, I'm only passing orders from *your* superior.'

The chauffeur with the window down hears him having met his kind before – the kind that shout back when they think things are safe for them – brakes suddenly and opens the door. The doorman makes to get out of there and run back into the safety of the Savoy. 'Come here you ******* flunkey git, I know your face. I'll see you again, and its . . .' He points at his eye, gets back in and sweeps off again.

Such is the olde world charm between one working man and his brother. That the one is the better of the other does little for working-class harmony that it yearns. Mind you, the jewel-splatted m'lady could have had the decency to tell her chauffeur herself instead of playing one off against the other. She knew what she was doing. The world today is not that different from then. Except the impression given by celebrity magazines and newspapers dangling carrots in front of us of an achievable high life for all. Never having to do a day's work. Do nothing and it will all come for nothing. I don't think so.

Got back to CVC at two. A queue had gathered around the lift. When it finally arrived, we all pile in. Someone hits the button, there was a clank and nothing else.

'Too many of us in here,' says the operator. He pushed the button twice more before opening the gates. 'Right three out.'

The gates were closed again. The button was pushed and this time the lift started up with its usual clank from the machinery. I was stood behind an enormous man who turned around and spoke to me.

'What's your name then?'

'Gil,' I replied.

He held out his hand to me. 'I'm Harold.'

Not only was the man enormous, but he had the biggest hands of anyone that I'd ever met, up until I went to Joe Bloom's boxing establishment to watch Sonny Liston being weighed-in. He walked right past me, a giant of a man, with hands like legs of beef. I thought Clay didn't stand a chance. But for the moment, Harold was the man.

'I'm the foundry room overseer, any help I can give you, just call me, only happy to help.'

'Thank you,' I said at the same time wondering what a foundry room overseer was, or even a foundry, and what one had to do with a composing room, I couldn't imagine. I asked George when I got back to my frame.

'Ah, Harold, Big Red, howya! howya! howya! A craftsman from the old school. You think six years is bad, they do nine.

12 – BIG RED

FOR PART of my education in hand composition it was necessary for me to understand the follow-up process. In this case it was not a press, but the foundry. It was there that I was to officially meet Harold the overseer; and the man known as Big Red.

He was standing in front of a bench with a large machined metal block on it. On this he had a lead plate about half the size of a broadsheet newspaper laying upside down. In one of his hands he held a thick punch type tool which had small dots of raised metal in its face. It looked something like a steak tenderising mallet. In his other hand, he held a hammer which he was using to make marks on the back of the plate. Having struck it a couple of times, he then turned it over and with another tool that resembled a pair of tongs he laid it over the reverse of the plate which I could see now was coated in copper and was an advertisement. He was gauging the thickness of the copper on the plate and scratching marks that needed to be proud or sunk. He then laid the plate down onto the metal block and commenced banging the punch again onto the back of the plate once again, which I could now see was becoming dotted with marks. To my astonishment he was actually measuring the difference to a thousandths of an inch the height between the plate and the surface he was laying it on, all the while making minor corrections with the punch. This is one of the most skilled operations that I have ever seen in the printing industry. George told me that there was a nine-year apprenticeship in the foundry; and with just that one skill, I was not surprised.

Harold explained to me the process to produce that plate. That of turning movable type onto a plate suitable for either printing or duplicating. Adverts produced here, as well as in similar ad-setting firms, are sent to newspapers and magazines around the country where they could be placed into their publications. A destructive process in that the advert, a forme of type with half-tone plates, having to undergo considerable pressures to produce a mould that molten lead can be poured into. That mould is known as a flong. Because of this destructive process, founders type being more expensive is not generally used unless the customer is prepared to pay for it to be destroyed, otherwise monotype, a cheaper alternative is used. The lead plate, depending on the number of impressions needed from printing, may be left in this state or hardened if a longer life is required. The hardening process is known as electroplating. This involve a thin copper surface being laid onto it.

He took me along to a vast machine which had a metal base like the stones we had in the comp room and pulled out a forme from a rack and placed it onto the surface. A full page advert that would go into a broadsheet newspaper was locked in its chase. He then placed a sheet of damp blue, that looked to me like cardboard over the forme and laid a blanket over it. Next, he produced a large brush and proceeded to beat it all over. This he told me was to create an impression in the cardboard. When the forme had had a thorough beating, the forme was pushed under a press. Harold pushed a button on the side and the bed of the machine was raised. A ram came down and began to push itself down onto the forme. After a while, the pressure was released, and the forme removed. The cardboard was taken off and turned over it revealing a perfect impression of the job in it. The advert had gone from wrong reading to right reading.

Asking me to follow him he took me further down into the foundry, here the cardboard impression was placed into an upright metal plate which was mounted in a frame. The covers of the frame were closed together. Then a ladle of molten lead was taken from a pot at the side and poured into the frame. There was a hiss and a bit of smoke. A few minutes later he opened the frame and there was laying underneath the piece of cardboard with a lead-plate image of the job again. This was the stereo plate. Wrong reading and ready for printing from. The mould could be used to produce any number of these should they be required. If, for instance, it was an advertising campaign designed for several national magazines or newspapers they could be sent out simultaneously for insertion. The stereo could now be made into a master, or for longer runs, where wear and tear would compromise the quality of the image it would be given a surface coating of copper by electro-plating.

Harold then took me into another room containing a large metal tank of electrolyte. A liquid solution of copper sulphates. Over this hung copper ingots. The plate was hung over a bar and connected to a clamp itself connected by a wire. He explained that the lead plate would take a positive charge while the copper ingot was the negative. Both lowered into the blue solution it started to slowly bubble. Now by a process known as electrolysis the copper atoms are taken from the ingot and transferred to the lead plate.

I must admit I had heard of the process from my chemistry lessons at school. Then it was how they put chrome onto bike spokes or car bumpers. But to see it being done was quite fascinating. It is the sort of thing that you cannot imagine could happen. But here, as far as I was concerned, it did indeed happen, and to good effect. The plate was left in the solution for quite some time, but Harold removed one that had been done earlier. There was a coating of copper all over it. This plate had now changed its name from stereo to electrode with the whole process being called electrotyping. Some minor adjustments to the surface by hitting the back with that steak tenderiser and it was finished. And that was what I saw Harold levelling up when I first went to see him.

And why did they call Harold, Big Red, I hear you ask?

Simply it was his ability to sink many, many pints of a keg beer known as Watney's Red Barrel at a single session. Popular at the time, Watney's decided to change the name of Red Barrel to just Watney's Red. Advertising was based on the Russian Revolution where advertising billboards showed Khrushchev, Mao and Castro all enjoying a pint of Watney's Red. The yeast being removed by filtration in its process, to be replaced with carbon dioxide, did away the need for hand-pumping and did nothing to enhance its flavour. It gained an absolutely terrible reputation for taste as drinker's palates improved, eventually becoming a beer that people would actively avoid.

13 – TRANSPORT AND ACCIDENTS WAITING TO HAPPEN

CANNOT quite remember where I got that Bown from. Most people have never heard of one. Everyone's heard of a Villiers engine though. It had one of those. The Bown itself, as a motorcycle, resembles nothing you will see on the roads these days – unless you're watching a vintage or veteran motorcycle rally, and even then, I doubt you'll see one. Nevertheless, it was a motorcycle in need of what one might loosely call – a restoration.

That is, it had a frame, tyres, an engine, a carburettor, and a coil. It had a back brake, but no front. It also had a clutch lever and a throttle. What it did lack however, was a petrol tank. And with its only means of motion being to push it down the garden, jump on and freewheel down the lawn, leaning it to one side before applying the footbrake; sliding it sideways, bringing it around on itself whilst maintaining balance in the opposite direction being as close as it came to mobility. For the moment, I thought, all quite harmless really. Dad wasn't very pleased about the state of the lawn. And with the other likelihood that I might overshoot and career through the greenhouse he suggested my getting rid of the bleeding thing. *Huh!* Parents eh! Tch! No faith in their off-spring. His fault really, as mum reminded him was, 'Taking him to speedway, what were you thinking of?'

She was right. Speedway was the inspiration for all this sliding with the Bown. Watching the Dons at Wimbledon sliding speedway bikes around the track; a fascination with which I kind of fancied the idea of doing in the evenings when I had finished work. Just another string to my bow. Dad was a St. John Ambulance man. And Wimbledon, on a Wednesday evening when the Dons were home, was his venue for putting into practice the principles of first aid according to St. John. Of course, he would get complimentary tickets for me.

Like some latter day gladiatorial games, the evening started with a procession of those involved. To music something akin to that of *Queen Of All The Fairies* (not its real title), first the officials: the referee's, timekeeper's and promoters, the track maintenance men, who would go around after each race with their tractor re-sweeping the track surface. All wore the uniform and colours of the club with matching berets. Next came the riders. The away team first, waving to their fans, then the home team, the Dons getting rapturous applause. Then dad. One of six St. John Ambulance men, wearing their white satchels, water bottles, carrying a stretcher; too far back to hear the music properly; all marching out of step.

The complimentary ticket would put me in the stands where I could sit in the warm, have a meal or a drink in comfort. But that wasn't for me. I would stand at the ringside so that I could get a whiff of the alcohol and the Castrol R oil from the bikes as they revved up under the starting wires, before being released like arrows from a bow. Back wheels trying to get traction as the bikes lifted their front wheels high into the air before taking off towards the first bend. Then all four riders, juxtaposed, leaning into the corner, metal boots scraping on the track, front wheels flexing side to side as riders fought gravity before the straight. Then flat out down the back straight before the next corner; coming so fast the riders literally threw the bikes over. A rider on the outside, holding it a mini second longer than the rest to gain advantage, could overtake. With only four laps there wasn't room for complacency if you weren't in front, and fortune favoured the brave. Make a mistake and you were in the wire fence. I saw a rider killed that way one evening. Halfway through the second lap in the time it took to read this sentence it was do or die! The stand stood and a roar of the crowd went up as each cheered his or her favourite, then the race was finished.

Next race. Another daring to overtake on the straight, does it, pushing the inside rider into the edge sending his wheel momentarily out of his grip. He holds off. There is another roar, then into the fourth. It's one on one now. Both go around the last bend together the outside man having to go faster, then it's into the last straight and the chequered flag. Nothing in it. They throttle back and shake each other's hand in mutual congratulations and respect, the other hand waving at the crowd like a latter day Spartan. The crowd go wild, and as quickly settle back for a drink, a smoke, and a fifteen minute wait before the next race. It's bare knuckle, raunchy and crude and satisfies ancient blood lusts; and as popular with the fairer sex as the males.

At the end of one meeting dad took me into the pits where

I could see the riders and their bikes. My heroes up close. Ronnie Moore, Peter Craven, Ove Funden. 'Fancy a go, son?' one said. *Did I?* Don't know who he was, thought he was joking, when I realised he wasn't I didn't need a second asking. A couple of the riders seeing the fun, stuck a pair of over-size boots and a helmet on me. The left boot weighed a ton. On this one boot the rider controlled the bike using it as a fulcrum to drive it flat-out into the corners at the same time controlling the back wheel in it slide. Sitting astride the Jap 350 single with one gear and no brakes, my heart was racing. They attached the engine cut-off lead to my wrist two of them pushed me out onto the track and let me go, one running alongside. I screwed open the throttle. The noise from the engine was deafening. The front wheel lifted, I shut the throttle down and it came back down with a thump, then it went away heading for the back straight like it had a mind of its own. The helmet – not my size – was hanging off the back of my head and around my neck now. There was no way I was going to get around that first bend, not without ending up in the wire safety fence. I managed to shut the throttle down which was not that easy with the forward momentum of the bike. I pulled in the clutch lever and stalled it. It stopped and everything went quiet. I-I-I was *hooked*.

Mum wasn't impressed when she found out. She was not one for the old two-wheels. Her brother – Alf – a Navy man; mentioned in dispatches after saving lives in a fire on his ship during the war, had an accident on his motorcycle back in the fifties. Well, to say it was an accident was missing the point. A lorry clipped him as he was going down Portsdown Hill in

Hampshire catapulting him through a telephone box. In one end and out the other; and all without the aid of a crash helmet. It would have been a good trick had he survived. They never did make large enough windows in those old red boxes. Anyway, as anyone with children will know, to try and keep a lad from a motorcycle is tantamount to holding back the tide. The upshot was, I soon tired of freewheeling and decided that the Villiers engine was due for a resurrection fire-up. And so, I collected the bits I needed for so to do.

Attaching a milk bottle full of petrol upside down with electrical tape to the bike's frame, the fitting of a rubber bung from one of my beer brewing jars (another story – another time), with the end of a siphon tube in the milk bottle the other to the carburettor the accelerant was sorted. Now for a spark. There was a spark plug fitted but no plug lead from the coil. Baring the wires from the lead I excitedly, with the electrical tape, attached it to the spark plug. I was ready. I put one of dad's old cheese-cutter hats on – back to front. Now for the moment of truth. I kicked it over a couple of times. It actually tried to start, but that was all. I decided that I should bump-start it down the garden – speedway fashion. So putting it into second gear and pulling in the clutch lever I pushed it getting up to about five miles an hour, then jumped on. Let go the clutch lever. It fired up and took off in the direction of our dad's greenhouse. I just about managed to steer it past and alongside it where it hit an old pear tree stump that had been sawn down a couple of years before. I was thrown into the mint patch up against our next door neighbour's fence while the milk bottle of petrol, mysteriously smashed, showering the spark plug lead with petrol. Dad's hat caught alight instead of my hair. There was a bit of an explosion. Well, bit more than that actually. As I said to dad at the time, 'It went up like the *Hinderberg*, you should have seen it. Don't know why you're complaining about a few broken and blackened panes of glass. Mum's had the best of the season from her tomato plants and they're all ruined. I don't know why you're worrying about them; I could have been *killed!*'

As Jerome K. Jerome so admirably put it in his book, *Three Men In A Boat,* the scene: *sans* tin-opener, that sees the character George holding a persistently refusing to open tin of pineapple between his knees; his co-conspirator, Harris, a sharp stone against its top lid, with the author holding, poised high, the boat's mast above his head, and with gathering strength and a rush of wind, bringing it down hard onto the stone.

It was dad's hat that saved *my* life that day.

My transport problems eventually became sorted when Keith sort of gave me his scooter. Well, loaned it to me to get back and forward to work. Think his new wife, Maureen, was concerned for his safety. *Keep death off the road* was never more an appropriate adage when I smacked L-plates on that piece of Italian machinery.

Christ! I don't think a week went by without my coming off it. Its side panels spent more time in CVC's foundry being hammered back flat by Harold than it did attached to the scooter. As for the skin on my arms and legs, well they were like a war zone, permanently stinging. Mind you, I could make it from Tooting to work in just over twenty minutes. Going through the Drain into Holborn at breakneck speed trying to hold it on the bend was something I aimed for, invariably losing my nerve at the last second, then scrapping along the tunnel wall kerb, both legs off the platform fighting for balance.

Mum, in her infinite wisdom somehow thought – for God alone knows what reason – that a scooter was, well, more of a tame mode of transport than a motorcycle, not likely to cause any injury to her son of any lasting nature. Which, up to a point, in Keith's case was true. She conveniently forgot that the majority of Keith's scars and injuries were the result of road race cycling for the Army. The only real accident he had on the scooter was when he went under Putney rail bridge on his way back from Maureen's one evening. Not seeing the malt slops on the road from one of Young's beer drays, he limped in covered in blood smelling like a brewery without having had a drink, saying to our dad, 'Worse than ice it was!'

He might have added one or two expletives, I wasn't there to hear. The problem with a scooter is its stability – or rather, lack of it. Due to the small diameter of its wheels being half the size of a motorcycle, when it comes to the wet, if you have to brake, it goes everywhere but in a straight line, as opposed to its bigger brother. A proper motorcycle, with skill, can be kept upright. I wanted a Triumph 500; mother was not to be persuaded. She had other ideas, it was Keith's Lambretta or nothing.

'And you're to take a test – *and get an helmet!*'

Now, as for the test, I'm not going to tell you the story

that's been going around London for half a century or more. Of, 'It's true, it was a mate of mine!' from the School of Kosher Pork Pies, as used by just about every wide boy *cum* yobbo the capital has given birth to. About how a motorcyclist on his test was told by the examiner that he would wait at a particular corner, and that he was to keep going until he (the examiner), would step out in front of him (the learner), at the appropriate time, and he (the learner), would do an emergency stop. No, I'm not going to tell you that yarn, 'cos it's a long story and appears even taller and ever more unbelievable with every exaggerated re-telling of it. Added to which you wouldn't believe me anyway 'cos I'm a Londoner prone to ostentations of histrionics (or *bull-shit* if you like). Suffice to say, that when the motorcyclist had inadvertently knocked the examiner down that had stepped out in front of him, with his hand in the air to indicate to the luckless examinee his need for him to make an emergency stop, our learner hadn't yet reached that particular point, it being another, who he had passed the week previously.

Honest governor, would I lie to you, it was a mate of mine. Or my brother, or my father, or uncle, aunt . . . *ad infinitum* . . . granny . . . oh, groan!

No, listen, this was *true*. When I took my test. No listen. Would I tell you a lie after all that? When I took my test, the examiner was standing outside Tooting Broadway Underground station when this guy jumped from the platform of a number 77 bus and I hit him. Knocked him straight down. And guess what, I still *passed!* The examiner said he was going to allow me a licence because it wasn't my fault that the guy jumped in front of me, adding to which I had kept the scooter upright. Probably the first time he'd ever seen that done. Now *there's* something to be said for taking a speedway bike around a track with oversize boots.

Coming soon to a cinema near you. Jackson purchases a shotgun and a box of cartridges!

14 – THE BEANO

BEANO/BEANFEAST: *n*: a once a year celebratory dinner with colleagues; synonymous with a quiet drink with friends; a convivial gathering together of collective minds for the furtherance of knowledge: to extend that knowledge for the greater good of all man-kind, that he might see the wonders of the Universe and the Glory of God.

A fine definition, though more often than not, a right good piss-up and all night brawl. A normal event in London, especially with printers and the like. For Hiram B. Good's Showboat and Print Fiasco. A much-celebrated, much castigated and very much inebriated floating mass of eccentric humanity on passage from the Bloody Tower to Sodden Southend on September 4th, 1965 was how this one fared.

A riverboat trip to the seaside was a once a year occasion for artisan's and their apprentices to let their hair down. (*George didn't have much.*)

'I heard that, Stonewall! Bit of respect for the dearly departed if you don't mind.'

Southend-on-Sea, being London's favoured choice for such an event, being closest to the sea and that, was decided upon. Which was just as well. There wouldn't have been many seaside towns that would have put up with the antics of drunken compositors bathing in their healing waters or sampling the bracing air of their spa as this Essex coast resort forty miles east of central London would have.

THE BEANO

The pleasure boat left Blackfriars' Pier 9.30 sharp. It was that punctual it left one of our party standing on the pier watching us cast off with us shouting, *Jump! Jump!* And he did, missing the boat by a good two inches – but was smack on for an appointment with the Thames. Names have been spared to protect the innocent.

One down. By 9.45 we were tucking into hot sausage rolls and the first drink of the day. Four crates of Watney Light Ale between us before disembarkation at Southend Pier. It wasn't the warmest of days and the combination of beer and a chill wind whipping up the Thames estuary: we were glad when we had had enough.

Southend-on-Sea isn't a Regis resort or a Spa town – although it does boast seven miles of seafront and the longest pleasure pier in the world. As for its healing waters it doesn't have any — not for nothing is the pier a mile long – mud aplenty though. When the tide goes out you can walk to Margate from Southend, although you might have to roll the old trousers up. No, what Southend boasted then were other attractions of which it could be justly proud.

Originally the southern end of the village of Prittlewell, Southend was home to a few poor fisherman huts and farms historically close to Prittlewell Priory. In the 1790s stagecoaches from London made it, although accessible, it was not until the coming of the railway in the 19th century that it began to take off as a popular seaside resort. It was then the pier was built. It was the fictional seaside location for the John Knightley family in *Emma* by Jane Austen, published in 1816.

The family preferring it to the Cromer some one hundred miles from London; compared with its easier distance of forty miles from the London home of John and Isabella Knightley.

The Kursaal (*By Its Dome It Is Known*), was one of the first ever theme parks in the world. It pre-dated Coney Island in America. It had its own ballroom and stage with entertainers to match. The Ted Heath Band, Cleo and Johnny Dankworth, to mention but a few, appeared there. Vera Lynn started her career there. Of course, the Kursaal meant, as far as I was concerned the Wall of Death and a chance to see the famous, Yvonne Stagg, Britain's first wall of death rider tanking a BSA 500 Twin Star around its 20-foot diameter bowl. Unfortunately, it was closed. Southend might not have been a spa town but the English for the German word Kursaal is *Cure All* or *Spa,* so it's not a million miles away from being one.

George had booked a restaurant where we could get kebabs and suggested that we might like to get a drink first. So off we all trooped to *The Saucy Sailor* public house. I mention public house just in case you might be thinking that the name was some sort of sobriquet for one of Her Majesty's Naval ratings. Southend certainly had its fair share of them. You could also be forgiven for thinking that they were called *Saucy Sailor* from the calling of them from the side alleys by the professional good time ladies trying to drag them in off the streets, to, I guess meet their mothers or save their souls. I don't know. Anyway. I digress. Into the *Saucy Sailor* we trooped and up to the bar before George called us away into a line. Ragged at first, but he was an ex-Royal Navy man, and soon had us paraded up and down getting us to stand to attention until he was happy, calling us to number from left to right. It ended at nineteen. He went to the bar. 'Nineteen pints of Guinness, landlord – and have one yourself.' He paid. Nineteen @ 1/9d a pint! £1. 13s. 3d. Nineteen pints of Guinness at today's London price of £3.60 a pint would cost £68.40. Plus, one for the landlord, £72. *Bargain!*

We put money into a kitty for another couple of rounds (apprentices were exempted), had a few more before setting off to our next port of call.

A Greek restaurant where kebabs on sticks were the order of the day with chips and wine. Delicious pieces of barbecued lamb with vegetables that melted in your mouth. Mind you, I wasn't impressed with the wine, even though at 6/8 a bottle it was supposed to be good for a Retsina. It did have a peculiar flavour though. George said that it was the Aleppo Pine resin in it that gave the wine its unique piquancy, adding that it has been made for 2000 years. I replied that at 6/8d a bottle, I don't care how old it was, I'll stick to fooling my gustatory nerve into believing that 1/9d a pint was the new 6/8d.

With just an hour to go to catch the tide and the boat back to Tower Bridge we all made off in a slow walk back to Southend Pier. A few more drinks on board before we arrived back at Tower Bridge and disembarked. I said that I thought that I might go home as I was feeling a little worse for wear drink-wise. George said that the answer to that was a bowl of jellied eels, an ideal cure-all for preventing a hangover. Some agreed, I wasn't so sure. The remainder thought as they had never eaten them before they'd give them a go. George suggested Tubby Isaacs in Aldgate, so off we went.

Still called Tubby Isaacs, although the man himself had emigrated to America in 1935, his stall taken over by his then assistant, Solomon Gritzman. Here we consumed a dozen cartons between the six of us. Two threw up at the sight of them, two threw up after eating them. George and I did not. I was brought up on the fish as was George and we both felt all the better for the eating of them. Here we parted company, deciding that we'd call it a day.

Derek, a close friend of mine, was a compositor apprenticed to a general trade house south of the Thames close to where we both lived, was one of the supporting cast invited to join us for the day. Making the decision to walk off the effects of the drink, we both decided to make our way back to Tooting by walking a little way to a Tube station closer to home. After half-an-hour I had an overwhelming urge to wring a couple of pints out of my bladder – as you do. Seeing a block of flats, I disappeared under a service area that held dustbins. It was dark. Going into a quiet corner I was just beginning to damp some old boxes and newspapers down when a voice came from between them.

'*Oi!* What the fuckin' 'ell's goin' on. You *dirty* bastard.'

The voice came from some old tramp that had settled down for the night. To have suddenly been awakened by an unwelcome shower of potassium and overspill he, being not impressed complained. I concurred with him, saying sorry. Starting to walk away, re-adjusting myself, I became aware he was coming after me. A lump of wood in his hand he was threatening blue murder. It turned out he wasn't as old as I first described. In fact, he was not much older than me at the time and it was touch and go whether he would catch me. Derek seeing what was happening egged me on to run faster where we didn't stop until we arrived at the Bank Tube station. Hurrying up to the ticket office I stated my destination.

HIRAM B. GOOD'S
SHOWBOAT and PRINT FIASCO

A much-celebrated, much castigated, much pixielated and very much inebriated floating mass of eccentric humanity on passage from the Bloody Tower to Sodden Southend on September 4th 1965.

OUR PERFORMING APP. **Gil. JACKO** Organizes (?) beanos, smokes cigars, sets type	"LIVELY LEN" **PASSEY** Half a night is better than none!
That Daredevil at the wheel !!! **VIC ("SKID-MARKS") HALL** This year: Brands's Hatch—next year: Colney Hatch!	**GIGGLY MARTIN** The poor man's Colonel Grivas.
MYNHEER (P.....ck) JACKSON CVC's Ambassador to the Low Countries	**'ATLAS' ABRAHALL** Weight for it—and Charge !
"BARGE-IN" **Tony Edwards** Moving in ever-decreasing circles until finally...	Supporting Cast D. TREADWAY - The Printer's Devil A. BRIDGE - - - - "Mr. Therm" P. CORBETT - - - "Black Netley"

'Two singles, Tooting Broadway, three bob,' the ticket officer said.

I started going through my pockets then looked at Derek. 'That's 1/6d each. Got any money?'

'Hang-on,' he replied going through his jacket. He was taking his time, with an expression on his face that he'd just spent his last half crown on eels.

My heart sank, 'Oh no. Not again,' I muttered to myself, fearing I would have a track record with the London Underground and be thrown out.

'*Half a crown!*' he said producing a silver coin from his pocket.

I could have kissed him.

15 – SWEARING AND OTHER TERMS OF ENDEARMENT

BAD LANGUAGE was rife in a printing office.

I'll rephrase that. Bad language is rife anywhere a group of men work together. The difference between them that are not part of the printing industry and those that are is a simple one. Printers. Compositors in particular are subjected to every form of copy presented to them from whatever source, for whatever reason, in the English language. In the course of setting copy a compositor will often come across a piece of bad grammar or a spelling mistake. In most cases he will correct this before continuing in spite of the simple rule: *Follow copy out the window*. The following of such a rule was that it was assumed that the author of a particular piece of copy was a man of education, of letters even. In some cases, he might well be. Whether he is or not it is not in the compositor's remit to assume one or other. The setting of type and presentation might be winkle bags or letterheads, and some might, going to the other extreme, be for a publications like *Music & Letters*, an academic high-brow publication by the Oxford University Press for musicians that play more than banjo ukuleles and mouth organs at their local pub on a Friday night. Not that there's anything wrong with that, but, there might just be the slim chance that the author of *Music & Letters*, will have the edge, English-grammar-wise, over the copy writer of the winkle bag or letterhead. The compositor, handling work from both the educated and the not so, would build into his own education a degree of English grammar and spelling that might, just, put both to shame. Correction and alteration of copy, with the aid of the head reader, would be carried out with scarce comment from either writer – putting down such correction as an oversight on their part due to the pressure of academic work or a queue at the winkle stall barrow.

Coming into the trade; and to help compositors in this quest for the furtherance of good English grammar certain publication are recommended like, *Fowler's*, an *Oxford English Dictionary*; a copy of *Roget's Thesaurus*, together with styles of house. Anything beyond that, a good printing reading room, with its shelves of reference books could well put a library to shame – well, nearly. On top of that, a good head reader is worth his weight in gold. A particular saying when it came to hand type-setting artisans was, *If you want to know how to spell a word, just ask a compositor; and if you want a second opinion ask his head reader.* And that, comes from the world of journalism.

So, having gone through all this diatribe about why bad language is rife in a printing office, and the reason it is *acceptable* is because the poor compositor, spending all his days righting and setting the English language, feels, at certain times, under stress and the right to express *Anglo Saxon* in all its most colourful forms in recognition of England's historicol and ancient past – *bollocks*, I've just spelt historical wrong! – is his damned right. Any questions?

16 – TWENTY-FOUR HOURS FROM TULSA

DURING my time at CVC the studio side expanded to meet an ever-growing demand from the advertising industry and to contain as much as it could in-house. Photographs of models for adverts were taken in our studio premises before being sent out for whatever process or media required. CVC opened its own studio downstairs from the comp room and for reasons best known to itself was out-of-bounds to us. It might have had something to do with the fact that models (girls) would arrive by taxi clad in whatever would be suitable to cover up what it was not suitable to show without the lens of a camera in front of them. This would inevitably lead to a rush from the frames to the windows and a cacophony of wolf-whistles and other such like noises in order to draw attention to the fact that there were men up here. The girls' being above such demonstrations of attentiveness from such a lower order would signify the fact with a V-sign or other such female trait affirming the reasons for the studio being out-of-bounds.

Of course, not all the models were girls. Actors and actresses turned up from time to time. The like of those that were currently in vogue in the promotion of adverts. Katie, of *Gives each meal man-appeal!* fame (Mary Holland) and Philip (Richard Clarke) of Oxo family fame were two of the most famous. We had a guy that worked one of the proofing presses who moonlighted on a stall in East Lane Market. He used to sell some of his wares at work: things like razors, shaving cream, aftershave; 'something for the weekend, sir?' In the winter he did a line in packet soups and Oxo cubes. Cold winter's day. Oxo cube scrunched up in a mug of hot water with a good seasoning of pepper – ideal! Of course, some of these Oxo cubes had passed there sell-by-date. Which was not strictly true, as there was no such thing then – more, if a food product looked inedible, disfigured by mould, or generally no longer fanciful, generally speaking, it would have found its own level in the sale ability stakes. Such were Oxo cubes at the end of the summer that had got hot then cold so many times they resembled something unmentionable inside their little silver cube when opened. Suffice to say that every time that Richard Clarke turned up in his Morris Minor and parked it up outside CVC it tended to get showered with the little brown droppings. If it's something that you still feel aggrieved, Mr. Clarke, I'll own up to being one of the culprits.

Occasionally CVC's studio would use some of the staff upstairs – some of the prettiest I hasten to add. Although one of the typist's was taken aback at first when it was discovered after she had gone down to be photographed that it was only for sporting a pair of shoes. Apparently, she had pretty feet. I never noticed them, but I did have a soft spot for her and dated her.

There was another occasion when they wanted a guy from the foundry of an older age with a rugged look. The one that was selected was well impressed until he found out it was for a before and after ad. He was the before.

The biggest occasion for us was when Gene Pitney turned up. He was doing a promotional campaign for Hepworth's the tailors and men's outfitters. On that occasion us apprentices were invited down into the studio where he was being photographed to meet him. We couldn't get him to sing though.

Not a visitor to CVC, but often walking past the building – Ras Prince Monolulu, the well-known racing tipster. Dressed as an African tribal king or prince, he was the most famous black man in England, until Mohammed Ali arrived from America. My nan took me to Epson racecourse once or twice, and there would be the man himself. Surrounded by a ring of people, attracted by his cry of, 'I've gotta horse!' He would then walk around the inside of the ring resplendent in his costume extolling the virtues of the winning horse that he had inside knowledge of. This would go on for half an hour when he would then stop and sell his 'I've gotta horse, the winner!' that was inside of an envelope. Of course, if you were lucky enough to get the envelope with the winner in it, as opposed to the other envelopes that carried the names of the also rans, Prince Monolulu, was as good as his word.

Of course, us boys seeing the colourful man walking up Earlham Street was an open invitation to shout his famous catch-phrase at him. He would laugh and wave back at us: ever the showman. Apparently already in hospital, he choked to death on a chocolate that someone had given him. That was in 1965.

17 – A SUSPECTED CRIMINAL FOR A DAY

KEITH AND I HAD AN interest apart from print, although, you could say it might be considered allied. Photography. He was the camera man; I was the processor. Much to the chagrin of Maureen, his wife, the centre of our empire was 29 Brightwell Crescent, where she gave over her kitchen *cum* bathroom for dishes of developer, fixer, enlarger and other paraphernalia.

We had decided that it would be a good idea to follow the London to Brighton veteran car race where we would get some rare pictures. The London to Brighton Veteran Car Run being the longest-running motoring event in the world, was first run in 1896. To qualify, cars must have been built before 1905. Keith had the idea that we were to take pictures as we rode alongside of them on his Lambretta. That would be a good trick, I told him, you trying to take pictures while riding the scooter at the same time. I, on the other hand, had visions of a sliding door Bedford Dormobile with he, hanging out the door photographing them from there. And, as luck would have it, one of the journeymen I worked with knew a mate, who knew a mate, who just happened to have one for sale.

Now, Denny – not his real name (it has been changed to protect the innocent, or nearly) – came from Peckham. Now Peckham, like Tooting, had a bit of a reputation them days.

Probably still has now, I don't know, but anyway, that was where nefarious characters like Denny made their livings with goods 'falling off the backs of lorries' along with various other activities that I won't immediately go into. Peckham, like other suburban areas of London, was generally poor and generally left to get on with it. The upshot was that if you ever needed anything, it could be got – cheap. Those of you that are familiar with *Only Fools And Horses* will have some little idea of living in those areas. 'You never have to lock your doors around here,' an old woman said to me when she was leaving her house to go shopping after I had happened to mention that she had left her key in the door. 'Everyone looks out for each other round here.' She was right about not having to worry that someone would come in and steal from her. Nobody had much of any worth to take in Peckham. Now if you happened to live in Hampstead – well, that would be an altogether different story. You'd need to lock your doors, fit a moat and drawbridge and man the barricades. If you thought about leaving a key in the door there, they'd not only let themselves in but jack the house up on wheels and take it away to a lock-up for a proper dismantlement job.

Anyway, I digress as usual. When I mentioned to Denny that evening in his local pub, along with some of these friends, when I was playing five-card brag with them, that I was looking for a van (I won fifteen pound by the way), it came up that such a vehicle had just come on the market and could be mine for – fifteen pound. (Coincidences were not my forte at that time.) I readily jumped at the chance and went for a spin in it with the seller I had just won the fifteen pound from. The steering box had a bit of slack, the handbrake could do with taking up; but it had the sliding door I craved and on the whole, it was okay, so I parted company with the cash. Or should I say, let him keep his losses.

Mum and dad weren't particularly impressed when I brought it home and they saw it, but as I said to them at the time, it would also do for my diving. I was beginning to acquire a lot of gear and trips to the coast as well as getting up to the *Oasis* for the Wednesday night sessions was putting a bit of strain on my diving buddy, Norman and his car. It was such a trip one Wednesday night that became somewhat memorable; leaving me with a lot to explain and the possibility of being arrested, charged, and imprisoned for being an accomplice to robbery of one of Her Majesty's Royal Mail vans.

Driving over Waterloo bridge, the engine started to stutter then gave up. I cruised to the left side of the bridge opposite the entrance to the Strand underpass known colloquially as the Drain. Taking the traffic from Waterloo Bridge under Aldwych and into Kingsway it was my route to the Oasis swimming pool in Endell Street close to CVC.

I locked the van and went to a phone box and called the police. That might have just been my saving grace. Having told them what had happened and that I would arrange to move it as soon as I could, which might be the following day. They seemed happy with this and thanked me for letting them know. In the meantime, they said they would send a car over to see if I might be causing an obstruction. As it happened, I was off the following day, so asked my friend Derek if he would be able to tow my van back that day. Derek, who had an MG TD sports car said it wouldn't be a problem. While I was taking my diving gear out to make my way to the club they turned up. The officer said it would be alright where it was, but to get it shifted as soon as I could. So off I went, diving bottle, valve, mask and flippers all in my large carry-all army sack up to the Oasis for Wednesday evening dive training.

The following day, me and Derek drove back up to London and to where the van was. As we were putting on a tow rope, I noticed that The Drain had been closed off and that a number of policemen were standing at its entrance. Smelling something wrong, not guessing it was anything to do with me, we got the tow rope fixed and I got behind the wheel. Derek pulled off just as I saw a couple of policemen running towards us waving from the entrance to the underpass. I feared that I might be up for some fine for illegally parking. Derek saw them and slowed down, while at the same time looking at me for some sign that I had seen the police waving at me. I shouted out to Derek to carry on and that it was probably nothing to do with us. Derek, seeing the road clear, pulled a U-Turn and drove off the entrance to the underpass where we continued back to Tooting, only snapping the tow rope twice. He did later have to get a new clutch fitted after he noticed it was starting to slip as we turned into Tooting Broadway.

Come Friday, and I'm back in work when George calls me down the comp room. It's Bow Street on the phone. Up goes a mighty roar from the journeymen as to what I'd been up to.

Oh! Bolloes, I thought. Taking the proffered phone from George I tentatively said, 'Hello.'

'You Gilbert Jackson?' the voice at the other end of the phone asked.

'Yes,' I answered, thinking perhaps that they just wanted confirmation that I had got my van home alright.

'Can you come down to the station, we've got some questions to put to you concerning a mail van robbery under the Strand underpass last evening?'

'*What!*'

'Anytime in the next two hours if you wouldn't mind. Ask for . . .'

I didn't get the rest of what he was saying, I was that stunned. *A mail robbery!*

'George. That was the police. They want me down Bow Street. Something about a robbery last night.'

George took up his *Daily Mail*. Opening it up at the appropriate page he fingers down the article getting me to read over him. I read, that a Royal Mail van carrying a large consignment of cash had been stopped from going across its intended route alongside the slip exit to the underpass on Wednesday night. They had (the robbers), apparently gone to slip road with the intention of putting road closed signs up in order to divert the mail van down the underpass. It seems they had blocked the road off. Here they worked in peace tying up the driver and his mate, breaking open the van and grabbing the cash. It went onto say that the Royal Mail van was on its way to Mount Pleasant sorting office and should not have gone down

A SUSPECTED CRIMINAL FOR A DAY

the underpass for security reasons; but had been forced to due to 'an old van in the road they had left to cause the mail van to divert down the Drain where the robbery was committed.'

I broke out in a sweat and looked at George, 'Oh, *bollocks!*'

When I told him that an officer from Bow Street wanted to interview me in connection with the robbery he replied, 'And were you?'

I looked at him. How could he think that of me? *Christ!* There's nothing of me. How could he think that I was a hoodlum; that I could organise a heist on the streets of London.

'Only joking,' George replied. 'Well, you'd better go down there and sort it out. Do you want me to come with you?'

'No. Thanks for the offer though.'

A police station is a daunting place at the best of times. When it involves you being a possible suspect it becomes even worse. They soon put my mind at ease when they mentioned that I was only there to help them with their inquiries. That just made it worse. You read things like that, don't you? When they have a person banged to rights and that they are helping the police with their inquiries you do wonder.

They asked me to go through the events leading to my breaking down. So, I'm sitting in an interview room in Bow Street nick trying to tell my side of the story. When I had almost convinced them of my innocence in all of this, they happened to ask who I had bought the van off. Naturally, the name of the guy had 'slipped' my mind. The thought of finishing up in the Thames with a concrete overcoat, or holding up the Hammersmith flyover, like the missing Ginger Marks, does nothing for remembering names. The police didn't need a memory recall from me after all, one look at the registration logbook told them all they needed to know. What they did need from me was how I knew the man and how much I had been paid to break down in that exact spot on Waterloo bridge. This cost me another two hours while they made further inquiries. When I was finally released – after I had satisfied them that I was completely innocent (of that at least) – they said they would need to speak to me again and not to leave the country.

To this day, the boys in blue at Bow Street haven't been in touch with me. Although, if I do get a knock on my door 50-odd years on, I pray it is the police and not Ginger Marks's overcoat tailor.

18 – AN OASIS IN LONDON

DOWN THE ROAD from Earlham Street was a swimming pool (it's still there), where in the heat of a London summer office workers and the like engaged in the activity of cooling down. London, with buildings that trapped the heat, the populace of some 13 million people suffering 30 degrees where the rest of the country might be managing with 20, made it unbearable for working in. Naturally, London's swimming pools became magnets.

Known as the Oasis, it had both an inside and outdoor pool side by side. With an hour's lunch time, it more than easily filled half of it; the second half, still time for a pint.

Three or four of us descended upon its cooling waters a couple of times a week. There was Norman, Dave, Gordon and me. One day, I noticed, on the wall an advertisement for the Holborn branch of the British Sub-Aqua Club. They were seeking members.

Now, let me just explain another interest of mine that I had carried with me since a small boy. A husband and wife team, with the name of Hans and Lotte Hass, had been my inspiration; their underwater activities using the aqualung had taken me hook line and sinker. Yes, I know that Jacques Cousteau and Emile Gagnan had found the method of breathing with the use of a demand valve; being opposite the lungs on ones back; but it was in those early days the husband and wife team of the

Hass's that had first brought aqualung diving to the attention of the masses through the medium of television. Cousteau was to come later.

Keith had furthered my enthusiasm by taking me to Gamages the department store in Holborn when I was ten or so, buying me the first of my diving equipment. It was what was known as System Hans Hass. A mask and flippers. I know, devotees call them fins – how *twee*. I call them flippers. And as I became an international diving instructor, that is what they are, so there.

The mask was cut from hard rubber with a thick rubber strap that had to be tight to the face to keep the water from leaking up your nose. The combination of hard rubber with the addition of water pressure resulted in a meaningful red ring around ones face from just below the nose to the hairline on the forehead. The flippers were not much better. Red cut marks across the instep and through the Achilles tendon, the result of both pieces of equipment looking as if they had been cut to shape with a bread knife. All in all, the injuries gave the impression of a not very comfortable sport to any onlooker. But I was young. And if you think that's bad just wait until I get to the wet suit.

And while Hans and Lotte stole the initial show, it was Jacques Cousteau that turned the tables. His book, *The Silent World*, was the bible then. I still have a copy to this day. Any youngsters out there interested in diving today can do worse than read it before coming into the sport. It is atmospheric, detailing the events leading up to Cousteau's forays into the undersea world; having to learn the dangers the hard way. I'm not suggesting for one moment that that is the way to go, but it does serve as a warning on how to conduct oneself in this, still a dangerous activity for the unwary and the untrained.

While looking at this advertisement for the BS-AC, I noticed that Norman and Dave were also looking. It said that the meeting night was on a Wednesday, and all three of us decided that we would give it a bash.

So, we turned up, swimming trunks and towels rolled neatly under our arms and presented ourselves to the secretary. We had to have a test. Isn't it always the way? You can't just get started. First test was to hold one's breath underwater for 30 seconds. Next, pick a brick up off the bottom of the pool and bring it to the surface six times. Then they strapped a blacked out mask to your face with a snorkel. Here you had to swim the length of the pool. This was to see if you suffered unduly from claustrophobia. More tests followed over the following weeks, with lectures on the physics and what happens to a body under pressure. The lectures were held at the Oporto public house, where we could comfortably sit and listen with a pint. Finally, with all three of us passing our basic training, we moved onto aqualung training and diving proper.

Owing to the damage that might be caused to the tiles at the bottom of the pool, aqualung training was carried out at Buckingham Palace Road swimming baths in Victoria. That is, as opposed to the swimming pool that's in Buckingham Palace. They wouldn't let us in there. Apparently, because of the age of the Buckingham Palace Road pool, the tiles were sturdier and less likely to crack than the ones in the Oasis when an aqualung bottle hit the bottom. That was the reason given to us anyway, though once you looked into the water, they were not exactly pristine. There was a shortage of diving instructors at that time, so training was carried out by a professional outfit. A company run by another husband and wife team, Don and Jean Shires. Their company, Blue Sea Divers became synonymous in the making of the underwater scenes for some of the James Bond films. Here they provided equipment such as underwater cameras and scooters. Some of the club members doubled for the actors in the underwater scenes. Jean was my instructor, and I'm immensely proud to say she trained me. A rarity in those days, as most diving instructors were usually ex-Naval divers. A rumour at the time was that Don, her husband, had been involved in training with Operation Frankton, the commando raid on German shipping in 1942. The name of the film, *The Cockleshell Heroes*, was taken from the code name operation Cockle.

All three of us made the grade and just had to carry out three open water and sea dives at various depths to qualify as Third Class. The first was in February 1969. Laughing Waters, near Dartford. And a laugh it wasn't. We turned up to find a thin layer of ice was across its surface on that frosty and misty Sunday morning when we talced ourselves up in preparation for the putting on of wet suits. For those of you that don't know, talk is chalk. None of your lined material here to aid the neoprene over the body. Borrowed, they had seen better days, but not much. They had more repaired holes than actual intact suit. Arms and crotch areas in particular, just came apart when the suit was stretched putting it on.

I was the first to go in with Norman. And with a 72 cubic foot bottle of compressed air on my back, my mask held on my face with the palm of my hand, I launched myself backwards in a perfect jack-knife into the black ice-layered lake with gay abandon. The shock to the system on that morning as I sank to the bottom of that muddy lake was something else. A wet suit is supposed to allow a thin layer of water to enter where it settles on the skin to be warmed by the body where it should stay. With water coming into the suit from underarms and crotch holes, any chance for that happening was going to be negligible. When I moved my legs, any warm water I had accumulated was pumped out with fresh iced water being sucked in. I froze, keeping all movement to the minimum before surfacing to await my buddy.

I lay on the surface waiting for Norman to join me. When he did, he snatched his mouthpiece out and screamed from the cold. His language was appalling. We reluctantly nodded and made the sign to each other that all was okay sunk into the lake and proceeded to swim underwater side by side, both of us clutching our arms to our chests trying to conserve what warmth we had before we died of hypothermia. Perch and roach swam in front of us at speed followed by the biggest pike I have ever seen. It took me by surprise, I thought at first it was a shark. We carried on swimming for what seemed like hours before we turned around and swam back to the bank. We were both stiff with cold and turning blue before we came out. We couldn't stop shaking as we tried to dry and dress in the back of Norman's van constantly stopping to wipe the snot from our faces that seems to go with divers. We had only been in the water nine minutes.

The sea dive was more enjoyable. A weekend in Swanage, Dorset. And not one for missing a business opportunity, I went around CVC taking orders for lobster. We stayed at a hotel and dived under the auspices of the Wright Brothers (a diving school not a flying one), who were stationed on the pier. Here you could get any equipment that money could buy as well as getting air tanks filled. They took ordinary members of the public on dives using a large tank that was installed on the pier and looked a lot like the one that Houdini had been chained into before making his miraculous escapes. When we got into the sea off the pier, I couldn't believe how beautiful it was – and warm. With only Laughing Waters as a comparison this was the Caribbean. I started looking for lobsters – like no one's been here before! It became apparent to me that perhaps fifteen was going to be a bit of a tall order. Reducing it to ten, then five, then one, before I was going to have to settle for fish and chips from the chippie along the front. I did find a crab though – Bob Wright cooked it for me – and I took it back to London. Mum was over the moon. The journeymen at CVC weren't. Some had organised lavish sea food dinner parties, convinced that not only would lobster be on the menu, but oyster, mussels, and other such exotica. Told to go out and buy something seaside-*ish* for the following morning tea-break to make amends I settled on a tin of snails in garlic butter from the Italian delicatessen in Earlham Street. Opening them before they saw the tin with the label of molluscs racing on the outside, I told them they were large winkles. I *think* they believed me.

One of the girls in our party who was training to be a marine biologist found a pipe fish which she brought out to study and sketch. She was keen, going back that same night, donning diving gear she went in off the pier to put it back from where she found it. Well it was the 'Sixties.

When during the early stages of our dive training, we were to have medical examinations and chest x-rays. Unfortunately, Dave, six-foot six of rowing excellence, was discovered to have a shadow over one of his lungs. Putting it down to his height; that he might have had a slight curvature of the spine, he submitted for a second x-ray. It was not good. He died of lung cancer two years later; the day before I was to be married.

Dave, I should like to dedicate this chapter to you. RIP.

19 – MUMPING: AN AUGMENT TO WAGES

AS I MENTIONED earlier, regarding augmenting meagre wages – reference, in my case the taking pecuniary advantage against London Transport – us apps were always looking for the next opportunity. Apart from the obvious, that of doing the odd business cards for mates, or small printing jobs that might earn the occasional shekel; and what was known as KDs (*see* the chapter on Printing Trade Terms), mumping type was a heavy earner bringing instant cash to hard-strapped apps.

Repro and ad-setting companies were springing up all over the West End and City of London in the 'Sixties to keep pace with the new demand for instant advertising campaigns. These companies took a lot of money in setting up. There was an entire comp room to be established. Stones, chases, furniture. Proofing presses – for the reproduction of perfect black type and half-tone impressions onto barrata, a paper that had a pure white surface coating of china clay. But the biggest expense by far was type, and not your bog standard monotype. Founders type.

Type is made from lead, tin and antimony. Monotype has a brittle white metallic element giving it its hardness. Founders, however, has more of this antimony than monotype. This gives it a hardness and durability, coupled with a sharp clean cut face is ideal for reproduction. It also has the added advantage of

MUMPING: AN AUGMENT TO WAGES

being able to be used several times more than monotype. The downside was, whereas in monotype it could be pressed under a foundry flong-maker and discarded after, the virtual destruction of founders type was a cost that had to be recouped when it came to making flongs for electrotyping. Advertising agencies, where money was not in question, accepted this destruction for the beauty of the look. The upshot was that a font of founders type, depleted by this destruction, needing replacing, was not readily available if needed soon after.

The finest type foundries were in Europe and America. Promoted by means of printed catalogues and sheets, which ad agency designers, ever looking for the latest typeface, were eager to get hold of could not so easily be bought over the counter as monotype. Ad-setting and repro houses keen to keep ahead of the game were constantly buying new type faces. Let's take one that was in vogue as an example. Venus. Venus came in Light, Medium, Demi-bold, Bold, Extra Bold. Condensed, Extra Condensed, Extra Bold Extended and so on. Sizes ranged from 6pt to 72pt. Then there was the italic versions. Venus alone could take three tall boys of cases. Add another fifty or so faces and you've some idea of the cost, to say nothing of the room they took up.

Differences in some typefaces were subtle to say the least. Just a word on type face recognition, and contrary to what you might think, not all compositors had a knack for it. Especially when you start getting down to the smaller sizes. Take Universe Medium and Grot 215. The difference to a layman would not be immediately apparent, its subtleness needs to be pointed out in that the capital letter R has a bend in its tail while the same letter in Grot is straight. The lower case y has a twist in its descender while Grots is straight. Looking at a whole page for comparison between the two faces there is a colour that is immediately recognised by an expert, but not a layman. Another example is that of Placard and Impact. I'm no expert, but I'm not bad. Providing the page is older than twenty-first century PCs with all their new faces.

The not so expensive monotype was used for standard text. Times, Plantin, Perpetua, Baskerville etc. were all available then as they are now, their destruction was not important. Founders was used for display headlines. All, including founders, are available on a modern pcs today. Then they were not. If an agency needed them from an ad-setter, there was no compromise. So how did ad-setters get over this problem? Simple, what they didn't have, they borrowed. From each other. A system was in place between friendly ad-setters to share, borrow, and steal these resources.

This borrowing became known in the trade as mumping. Many of the new proprietors setting up were compositors themselves, part of a wide circle of friends and acquaintances, often having worked with each other before setting up on their own. This is where the firm's storeman came into his own. A compositor that turned storeman had to have a wide knowledge where type face recognition was concerned. He would have a visit from another firm, another compositor, who might need a couple of characters to make up an ad. So, the storeman would go to the case and see what he had. If it were a type face that was currently in vogue then he would need to go to the frame that contained all the work that had recently been dismantled waiting to be dissed back into its case. He would then look for the characters needed. It might be our old friend Venus. Star Illustrations, a company I had friends working for in Wardour Street, would need say an e, four f's, a cap W in Extra Bold Extended. Finding them our storeman, we'll call him Ken, would wrap them up in a piece of brown paper and put a rubber band around them. He would then go to his book, look up Star Illustrations, and put down the type that they had borrowed that day and date it. The comp from Star would then say, thank you, before returning to his firm. All very well if the firm was close. Say, within a couple of hundred yards of each other. Not so when they might be four miles away. This is where the apprentice came into his own. Known as a 'mumper' he would need to have a more than working knowledge of London, as well as the underground train routes to get there as quickly as he could if he was to make serious money. With a firm a little way a way he would invariably be given a taxi fare. Of course, he wouldn't use a taxi, far too expensive, he would take tubes, buses, and run. And the difference between a taxi and other modes of transport was, *cash in the bin*.

The working knowledge of getting from A to B; the ability to run between stations, knowing which line was going to be the least time consuming at any particular time of day was imperative. Of course, the firm knew what was going on, and provided you didn't take longer than a taxi – nothing was ever said. Steaming in out of the lift, having gone half across London, in the time a taxi would take, or less. Sweating like a pig and smelling like a Javanese wrestler's jockstrap, breath coming in gasps, I would return and walk down the comp room as casual as I could, the envelope with half a dozen odd characters would be handed over to the storeman who would book them in. I would then disappear out into the wash-room and collapse my head into a bowl of cold water before drying myself off and getting a cup of tea. All that for six bob. But that was a lot of money in the 'Sixties.

Of course, there were other advantages. People got to know you, where you worked, how you were doing. Net-

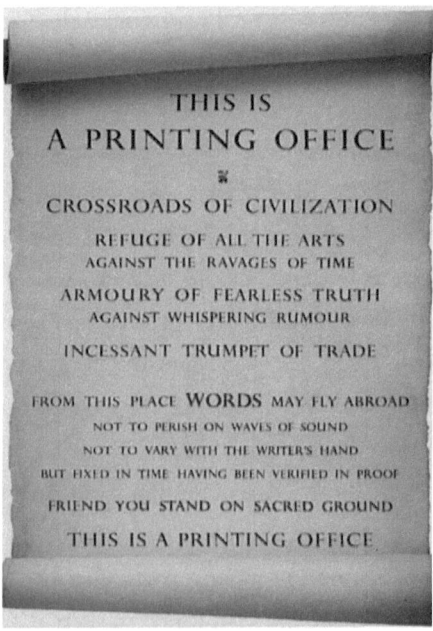

working you would call it today, and every bit as invaluable then as today. You got to know who was paying what, how much

MUMPING: AN AUGMENT TO WAGES

overtime, what campaigns particular firms were involved in. Not all that useful if you still had a couple of years before coming 'out of your time'. But useful for all that. Information went around our inner circle. An inner circle that became an even tighter closed shop. For only those that were in advertising and repro stood a chance of getting employment in it. Word of mouth was everything when someone fancied a change. Another ad-setting house might have just started up and were paying more. Or, as is the case of new start-ups, had more overtime on offer than the one you were currently working.

Not all type was borrowed, some was actually bought, and a trip to Red Lion Square off Fleet Street was another of the mumpers' destinations. Here could be found one of the biggest suppliers of trade type in London. Yendalls had the franchise from Riscatype, a Welsh type founders. This part of London I craved, for I felt I was part of something that was bigger than life itself. Here was one of my favourite destinations; the centre of the newspaper world, Fleet Street. Yendalls supplied packets of type over the counter. On one of the walls was a poster extolling the virtues of the printed word. These were stirring words to a young lad at the start of his apprenticeship. (And are to me still). Fleet Street was the centre of 300 years of newspaper history. All was about to change though, and very few of us saw it coming, apart that was from Robert Willis, one time secretary of the London Typographical Society, in his controversial publication, *The Changing Face of Print*.

An ending to it all that we thought so far away, was nigher than we realised.

20 – THE CAT

BY THE TIME most people arise from their beds, Covent Garden along with most other wholesale markets have finished trading for the day. From around 4 am market traders mysteriously evaporate into the public houses that are legally open for their benefit. (That is, open for *their* benefit.) Here a trader can while away half-an-hour discussing business with other like-minded traders with a pint, a bacon sandwich, and a smoke before finishing their work for the day. For this is what is known as the Dracula hours, where from midnight porters, buyers, and sellers transacted their business, moving the wares of whatever market they happen to specialise.

Old Billingsgate was fish, Smithfield meat. Covent Garden fruit, vegetables and flowers. Leadenhall, general food. Now these hours, happily coincided with the publishing of many of the newspaper and magazine publishers and printers. Odhams and Fleet Street for instance. All these establishments were close to markets; and of course, markets had drinking establishments that operated outside hours enjoyed by the general public in that they were open to cater for these market traders. Note again, I made no mention of printers being included outside of normal licensing hours. Neither, as in the case of Smithfield or Covent Garden did I make any mention of the Bow Street Runners or any other police station close to any particular wholesale market. Nevertheless, anywhere that the police exercised what they saw as their entitlement while at the same time using it as an excuse for keeping an eye on things, then others were bound to follow. Villains and printers, not out of any sense of brothers-in-arms you understand, came into this category of being able to pop-in for a swift half. All in all, customers, that no landlord worth his salt was going to question too closely their occupations, or from which market those occupations were exercised. With that in mind, drinking in those hours before even farmers begin milking for the day, was a right mix. Here anything could be got; and anything done by three groups of the widest and wisest boys in a unison of brotherhood and mutual understanding, without straying too far over the line that might be construed as criminal activity by speaking too loudly at the bar. For it was here that I fell into the bad ways of drink.

Drinking two or three pints in one of those market pubs (I'm sorry, but my mentioning of the antics during those heady days, precludes me from mentioning any names of establishments), after finishing our own shifts as ad-setters, I then made my way back to Tooting in time for opening time of 10.30 am at Jack Beard's for another couple of pints (I can mention that establishment because nothing untoward ever happened in there). Few people knew then that Jack Beard's was the colloquial name for what was in fact the Forester's Arms. Apparently, Jack was a a 19th century landlord that was held in some sway for helping people outside onto the pavement when they got slightly carried away the worse for liquor. A good Christian man he would show these people the folly of their ways, helping them onto the path of righteousness and the ways of the Lord with a swift kicking. I believe it still exists and is now called The Antelope. I must go back there someday. Anyway, I digress once again. Eleven am it's time to leave the Forester's and get on down to the Mitre for their opening time. A close family establishment; mum moonlighted there as a barmaid for many years. Here another couple of pints were ingested, then home, now worse for wear. Come five pm, then it was in for another swift, this time with my girlfriend Rita (the current Mrs. Jackson) to the Surrey Arms in Mitcham, before returning back to London to begin my 8 pm shift. Come 11 pm, a twenty minute meal break, over to the Nags Head for another couple, before finishing night shift and returning to the market to begin the whole cycle again. Don't talk to me about drinking and driving. When I came out of my time, I'm ashamed to say, I drove an MGA backwards and forwards to work with one eye shut to keep focus on the road.

Anyway, this chapter is titled The Cat, and I suppose that many of you readers have forgotten by now, what with my rambling on, wondering what all this has all to do with markets. Well, this early morning nonsense was also the time of the day when Mathilda and her daughter had finished their night's work of mousing and ratting. Strolling one after the other through Covent Garden market passing by *The Royal Opera House*, eyes darting to and fro, wary of human contact, were heading for home. For although Mathilda was getting on in years, and not as quick as she used to be, her daughter kept vigil.

The traders' hardly gave them a second glance, they were part of the market these two girls; indeed, they were openly encouraged and recognised for the job they did. And they were cheap. For the odd bowl of Kit-E-Kat and a saucer of milk, the rats and mice were kept, with others of their breed, in check. For Covent Garden, as other markets are a third plague in waiting: and have been since the Romans and will be still when man has wiped himself out.

Mathilda was half ginger, half tortoiseshell, and as close to feral as it's possible to be without being captured and tipped into a vat of wet cement. You wouldn't stroke her, not if you wanted to queue up in casualty for a couple of hours to have a tetanus jab. Her daughter, father unknown – had similar markings excepting for the black streak-like lightning bolt that shot through her left eye – would carry on the trade that she had learnt from her mother; clinging to her not out of any sense of love, but of a necessity to survive by example. With the light of day approaching they would sleep until night came once again. Their hotel, below CVC, among the paper sacks and fruit boxes with others needing a fixed abode from the weather. The methos, vagrants, and illegal immigrants. Children that had been abandoned (Dickens would turn in his grave), the odd drunk that had missed his last tube train home. All were welcome. And with a hot air ducting systems blowing down from its roof, all were warm.

Mathilda had one last job. Making her way into Earlham Street, crossing the square where the first showing of *Punch and Judy* was performed, she went under a snack van. The grease from the day before's burgers, fried eggs and sausages along with dregs of scrap vegetables and staling bread clinging to the road; with cooking oil dripping from a leak in the floor of the van being all around her she would mop up any edible, and not so, remains. Also, under the van was the odd saucepan that had been put there to cool until morning alongside empty tins of beans that had been overlooked and rolled under – and of course, there was the large frying pan. The inspirational kitchen utensil for Sam's best fried egg sandwiches, bacon and tomato rolls; all the talk of the offices and places of work in that area known as Seven Dials, meant nothing to Mathilda, as it hadn't done to her mother before her. And now, watched by her own daughter, who would go on to follow the feline family trait that had made Sam's *The Best Fried Egg And Bacon Sandwiches In The World*, she cocked her leg and urinated right into the middle of the frying pan before getting her head down for the night.

Sometime after I came out of my time, my friend Derek and me were at a loose end. It was New Year's eve, and we had trawled around the West End, drinking hither and thither before finishing up in the *Opera Tavern* in Covent Garden. Not overly busy for a New Year's eve being off the bitten track, it was mainly locals that gave it a nice friendly atmosphere that night. After celebrating with complete strangers, kissing and shaking everyone's hands, and with the sounds of *Auld Lang Syne* ringing in our ears, we said our goodbyes and made our way back up Earlham Street towards Leicester Square tube station, passing Sam's van as we went. Having got used to seeing it there, I really didn't take that much notice of it. It was Derek that drew my attention.

THE CAT

'*Look at that!*' he said pointing toward the van on the other side of the street.

'What about it?' I replied.

'That, over there. That cat. I just watched it, it's eyes followed you all the way up the road from the corner, then just as we got opposite, it came out for a closer look.'

A cat, half ginger, half tortoiseshell, with a black streak down through her left eye, was now poking its head out at me.

'Well, I'll be damned,' he continued, 'it seems to be looking at you grinning, like it knows you.'

And it did. Buying grub from the van for the lads every morning for six years must have made me familiar. It was staring straight at me with the grin of the literary Cheshire.

21 – TIMES UP

MIXED FEELINGS was my emotion then. For an apprentice, whatever trade, the ambition is to shed the chains of being an employer's apprentice. Not out of any sense of being treated badly – for I had been fortunate to have been surrounded by good men through the six years – more out of a sense of loss of something that will never be the same again.

The loss at a comparatively young age of our (and here I speak for Bruce when I use the word) mentor, George Good, who died of a heart attack two years before I came out of my time. A tragic loss to the printing industry of a dedicated man and overseer.

Responsibility was now on my shoulders for the first time in my life. Quite literally. The sense of it was overwhelming, and not a little worrying. For tomorrow I was to go from being a boy to a man. From an apprentice to a journeyman. And the shedding of my apprentice chains, that had all these years appeared to be something looked on with eagerness and bravado suddenly loomed frightening.

I was to be 'banged-out' Wednesday and leave Friday for pastures new. Not leaving because I was forced to, but because it was considered that as long as an apprentice stayed put in the print office that he had been indentured, then he would always still be 'the boy'. So, I had grasped the nettle and taken a job with a general trade company, in Waterloo called *Kelleher, Hudson and Kearns.* A printers that according to my mum had employed my grandfather, although I haven't been able to ascertain the truth of that. But before all of this, I had the little matter of being 'banged-out' to contemplate.

Traditionally when a journeyman leaves his employment with a printer he is 'banged-out'. This being the holding of metal galleys in the air by his erstwhile friends and colleagues, the latter banging them with lumps of clump as they walk the length of the comp room and out the door. The noise can be heard for miles, and anyone passing below familiar with the ways of printers and compositors would know immediately what was going on.

Unfortunately, when an apprentice is 'banged-out' it is treated a little differently. And no, they don't use bigger galleys – or bigger clumps. London print shops had taken to borrowing some of the traditional methods meted out to apprentice coopers, with the emphasis on the messy end of the proceedings. Suffice to say, that for the previous year, I had been primed to the attributes of bronze-blue ink being applied to certain quarters of one's anatomy. Bronze-blue, not for any particular colourful properties that it may have, although anyone that's been to London Zoo and seen the arse-end of baboons, might consider it to have, certain, artistic merits. No. It was its sticking properties and its unique inability for removal before, perhaps, ones wedding day, which might still be some time off. 'Five years, it can still be there after five years?' I had shakenly remarked to one journeyman after I had plucked up the courage to speak of the matter. He shrugged and pulled a face: 'Could be – it's been known.'

Other stories to strike terror into an apprentice awaiting his 'banging-out' did the rounds. Like the one about an apprentice that had been 'banged-out'; his fellow journeymen feeling the need to 'finish off the page', had put him into a GPO mail bag and shut him into the goods wagon of a London–Penzance bound night train. Released by British Rail police, after the calling of help had finally got on a lady passenger's nerves who after two hours decided that she had better mention it to someone. The poor unfortunate, after finally getting his freedom; getting to breathe night air a little way up the line from Camborne in deepest Cornwall, was heard to ask of the railway police if they were sure this was his stop, only he thought that Finchley Station was still part of the London Underground system and what was it doing out in the open.

Another lad (where did they get all those mail sacks?), dropped into one, was attached to a crane on a building site, before being hand-winched up into the night air in what is now the finished remains of the Gherkin Building. The City police were none too pleased with that traditional occasion. The cable had come off its windlass, the mail sack had started to split: the plucky lad had brought along his pen knife to make what he thought was going to be a miraculous escape in a Houdini-like spectacle not realising he was 30 feet off the ground. The London Fire brigade was called out from Cannon Street. Spreading a net below the budding artiste just in time. A communal shout of *Olé!!!* could be heard in the darkness from behind a wall as he bounced safely into the net.

Came the day, came the man; I was, to say the least, not without feelings of some trepidation. Wearing my worst clothes for the *event* I made my way down the comp room to the offices and up the stairs to the managing director's office. Here I was presented with my indenture. Harry Heck was a man of few words. He shook my hand, bid me good luck, stuck a cigar into his mouth and waved me out the door, and on my way.

Not being able to face what was to come I decided to do a runner. Discretion being the better part of valour and all that, I would creep down the back stairs, through an unused exit, and out via the stage door of the Donmar. Unfortunately, what the other men didn't know about the layout of the building was more than made up for with Bruce's – he had all exits more than adequately covered. Accepting the window (three floors up) I could see that this was going to be a lost cause and I surrendered to my fate.

A large metal tank on wheels that we used for transferring the old metal down the stairs when the scrap man came had been made passably comfortable for me. It had a back rest and a wooden plank on its inside that was the seat. Lifted and dropped in unceremoniously, I was tied in and wheeled into the foundry. Here Bruce (I shall come back for him in two weeks' time), waited, a large can of black molasses in one hand and a wooden spoon in the other. He then proceeded to pour and scrape the contents over my head. Then came the sawdust, swiftly followed by buckets of drain gulley water from the fruit market. Already stinking like a London plague, I was then wheeled into the lift. Thank God, I thought, they haven't any bronze-blue ink. Oh, thee, of little faith. Paul Fishman, the proofing pressman was on hand with a large tin of the stuff. I didn't think that it had somehow been lost, as someone had mentioned that it had a couple of days before, as he was fully prepared with a pair of rubber gloves and a palette knife as an accompaniment. I started to struggle, but all in vain, I was bound tighter than a camel's arse in a sandstorm. One of the foundry men had hold of me and pulled my trousers open. Fortunately, I had the sense to wear a pair of swimming Speedos. Did that do any good, did it *b-b-b******s*. They came down as quick as the trousers. The palette knife came in with about half a pound of the bronze-blue on the end of it right up the middle of my nether region. Then, with the gloves he went to work with a goodly spreading motion, helping himself to more from the tin just to finish off, so to speak. 'There!' he said looking at his work, 'When that dries, they'll buff up a treat and shine like a couple of snooker balls. *Five points each!*'

I had been baboon-arsed, front, and back good and proper. The doors of the lift were closed, where we then descended to the Fyffes ripening area then taken out into the fresh air of Earlham Street. Thinking it was all over, I started to get myself out, but they had other ideas. A hand pushed me back into the metal tank before I was pushed with cheering escort up to the Seven Dials where the Greek and Italian food stalls; their proprietors that had come to know me over the years for buying their wares cheered as we rolled by. All those people that I had cheeked the last five years were going to get their revenge. All those salami rolls I had bought from these immigrants, and here they all were, joining in at this spectacle of Englishness by throwing all the old food they had into the tank, just to add to the flavour of the occasion. It didn't stop there as I thought it surely must now, I thought. No, it was through Seven Dials and on up to Cambridge Circus. Surely, they were not going to take this banging-out further than this. The images I had in my mind of other apprentices finishing up in Cornwall or hanging from crane hooks entered my mind and I began to feel afraid. Not only that but it was a cold day, and I was beginning to feel it. All I was wearing was a ragged shirt and my Speedos. The contents of the tin of bronze-blue, gave me the appearance of some super stud, which in better times I would not have been disappointed. But these weren't we were heading down the Charing X road. Here we were now joined by journeymen and apprentices from the other repro houses in Soho and district. Even the police, stopping to see what all the fuss was about, brought a sense of relief to me that this would surely come to end now, realising what was going on; nodded approvingly before going on their way. God, there must have been fifty or more of us, and it looked as if they were heading me towards Trafalgar Square. Suddenly they stopped. We were at Leicester Square tube station. Here I was taken out and tied to a lamp-post. Then with a cheer, they pushed the tank back the way we had come leaving me to my fate and London for an audience.

It was ten minutes before I managed to release myself. And with my Speedos packing their blue message; my ragged shirt;

I gathered together what dignity I could muster and made my way back to CVC through a throng of office workers, shop assistants, girls with minis, Costermongers and market people.

The foundry did their bit for the clean-up operation. After a good wiping down with Swarfega; and with the wiring disconnected I was lifted into an empty electrotype tank. I was then hosed down with a high-pressure jet washer, and in fifteen minutes I was shining like a new baby boy that had dropped a navy blue rattle own between his legs.

Glowing like a lobster, I put a clean shirt on. Keith had suggested that I take a change of clothes with me along with my new suit (mohair of course). From here I was taken to the Endel Arms where drinks and a buffet had been laid on for me. Keith came in after his shift and commenting to Lenny Weinstein that he hoped a thorough job had been done. All agreed that it had.

By four o'clock, having consumed rather a large quantity of Red Barrel that had been forced down my neck, I had a touch of paralytic dementia. Keith decided that it was probably best if I call it a day. Putting me on the back of his Lambretta, telling me to hold on tight to the pillion strap and not to let go, we rode off home. I didn't remember much of the journey, except for being sick with Keith having to keep stopping to let me off. I think we had to stop at Vauxhall, Clapham Common, then Balham High Road, not forgetting Tooting Broadway, where I decorated the side of the police telephone box in the middle by the statue of King Edward VII, each time Keith having to lift me back on to the scooter as I had a penchant for wandering off singing: ♫ *Jeeee'sus Wants Me For A Sunbeam* ♫ —

22 – THE LINE IS CUT

I'M GUESSING that the number of separate unions within the printing industry in the 'Sixties must have amounted to about a dozen or more; and at one time in the history of printing every craft had their own. Each was autonomous and jealous in the protection of its craft and the journeymen members working within it. Inevitably as each moved forward with the result of modernisation it was clear that some sort of overseeing organisation was needed. In 1890 the Printing & Kindred Trades Federation was formed with this in mind.

As an example, those involved with collating sections of books and publications, guillotining reams of paper to size and known as binders came under the National Union of Printing, Bookbinding and Paperworkers; passing and receiving of information over the 'wire' was known as the National Union of Press Telegraphists. Reporters and sub-editors came under the National Union of Journalists; Society of Lithographic Artists, Designers, Engravers & Process Workers (SLADE) were railroaded into membership of the union considered protection from their bosses a side issue to what was really happening to them, namely members' protection from the union threatening to black them if they did not fall into line. Mechanical typesetting machinery came under the Monotype Casters and Typefounders' Society; readers, the Association of

Correctors of the Press (I was a member for a short time while affiliated to the National Graphical Association); National Society of Operative Printers and Assistants (known colloquially as NATSOPA later SOGAT) became the biggest, and arguably the most powerful owing to it being allied to most other crafts. Although they were not technically craftsmen in their own right, many were assistants on presses or in the bindery that could and did usurp their influence against the proprietors and other union interests. In Fleet Street for instance you couldn't start a press without a member of SOGAT being present. That is not to say that they weren't essential – they were, but they did get a little out of hand in London when it came to newspaper production. Then there was my lot. Originally the London Society of Compositors, with its sister outside of London, the Society of Compositors, later to become the Typographical Association. The LSC became the London Typographical Society amalgamating with the TA in 1964 becoming known as the National Graphical Association. Most other small unions like SLADE and the Association of Correctors at Press, Electrotypers and Stereotypers had by that time been absorbed into the NGA. Print unions were centred in London with agreements made there affecting the whole of the country. The endeavours of the union to protect its members, in my view, came to an end in the 1980s with the introduction of new methods that had been knocking at the door with various new technologies each one superseding the other within a year or two; such was the speed of change. The old family proprietors like the Harmsworth's

(*Daily Mail*) and the Beaverbrook's (*Daily Express*) gave way to a new breed. Men like the Australian/American, Rupert Murdock; the Czech-born, Robert Maxwell (*Daily Mirror*) and the Canadian, Conrad Black (*Daily Telegraph*) – two out of three crooks! – came with the idea that they could release the grip that the unions had on the newspaper trade with the help of labour laws. With the help of Rupert Murdock, with his young pretender, Eddy Shah, his Media company, and Margaret Thatcher's Industrial Laws, together with the subsequent three year Warrington industrial dispute nailed Fleet Street for good. An agreement between the NGA and *The Times* management to switch from hot-metal to computer typesetting was soon followed by the other newspapers and Canary Wharf became the new Fleet Street. Once the news trade had got its freedom it was only a matter of time before nationally the printing industry went the same way. By the mid-eighties it was all but over.

Was it a good thing? As the man said you can't stand in the way of progress; and as far as my trade was concerned lead soldiers became old soldiers. Anyone with five fingers on each hand could operate a keyboard and a computer to produce pages of type that a printing plate could be made from. Although, the technical look of the printed page does leave a lot to be desired against what it was – it was good enough for a new generation of publishers.

Nothing they say is forever, although, when electricity finally gives up, I've still got my sticks and the ability to set a line of type. The only good thing to come out of it was that compositors – like their brothers in the mines that suffered the black lung disease: anthracnosis – would no longer be susceptible to the raft of mental and physical disabilities resulting from exposure to lead.

When I came into the trade, both my mother, her mother and my sister were in the bindery. My mum was a Mother of the Chapel. My brother, Keith was a Machine Minder Manager who had been apprenticed at Speights. He went on to become a member of the National Executive for the NGA. My uncle, Vic was a NATSOPA member at Odhams; I became, later, both a Clerk and a Father of the Chapel. My dad, fortunately not in the print, but an engineer – was Shop Steward. So, having come from a line of union activists I feel that I can say that, in the case of the printing trades', the unions' were blinkered in the coming of the *Spinning Jenny and* had learned nothing from history. They had the opportunity to take themselves and us into the new technologies if they could ever have broken the intransigence of The House of NGA/NATSOPA, Fleet Street Branch.

The collective noun for a group of compositors is a Chapel and their gatherings were naturally called, Chapel meetings. And Craske, Vaus and Crampton's were usually conducted in the upstairs of *The Nag's Head*, in Covent Garden. A pint accompanied each member as he went up the stairs – then down again for refills as the meeting progressed. Proper Minutes' and procedures were strictly followed. Everyone knew their place and when to have their say. Motions could be put; then amendments were added before the vote. Amendments were voted on first, and then the motion. The meeting was chaired by the Clerk to the Chapel, and although he was not the man that was the mouth-piece to the bosses, he was technically the top dog. Then came the Father of the Chapel, then came the Treasurer. And finally, the Minute taker. All very democratic – all becoming raucous as the evening progressed.

Meetings started out with a minutes' silence for any passing of brothers. Then the Clerk would call for the Minute taker to give a general resume of the previous Minutes before asking for acceptance in the form of a seconder and then a show of hands in favour of their acceptance.

Up stands Mr. Clerk, 'Thank you, I'll take that as an acceptance of the last minutes. Mr. Treasurer, could we have your report, please?'

The Treasurer stands and begins to read out the monies taken in, expenses, cash in hand, cash in bank and usually asks for a donation to our brothers in some obscure organisation that is being done down in Brazil by a company (usually British), that's chopping trees down depriving the indigenous population of a means of shelter and sustenance for their families. Then the Father of the Chapel is invited to address the meeting. He stands and then looks around the floor staring into each man's eyes. A new man this. A member of the Communist Party and supporter of the Russian Revolution and all things Red: Arthur Scargil to mention but a few. This new man taking the job a lot more seriously than his predecessor, begins:

'I'm perturbed that for the third time, having been to see

the management about getting time and a half additional money for late campaigns. That is, campaigns that come in of a Friday afternoon where we are then called upon to work at a moment's notice . . . it's time, brothers, to make a stand . . .'

Now I must hasten to mention here that the majority of printers – with an emphasis on compositors, are by nature, a money-grabbing, half a night's better than none, any chance of a Sunday, notwithstanding a double-ender shift before it, and a brigade of overtime rota-orientated men that would rather put off going to their grandmother's funeral if extra work stood in the way of the black-plumed horses that were being harnessed up outside the Co-ops undertaking emporium in readiness. And as for asking to take industrial action that would in any way jeopardise such arrangements with the management that might call for any additional hours at the drop of an hat – any hours, any time of the day or night including Christmas morning – an FOC might as well ask the very stone itself to bleed for all the good it would do him.

'Is that time and half a call-out payment in addition to hours worked?' shouts one of the lads. 'Get it if you can, but we'll not come out for it!'

The Father ignores the remark as he hasn't finished speaking on the subject in its fullness yet. '. . . I have been in touch with head office and have been given an edict . . .'

Here the chapel members all look at each other and start to mutter. The pints that they brought up to the meeting with them are starting to oil the machinery. The word *Edict* starts to be muted around. Now these are not simple men, but they do like plain speaking. One brave soul pipes up, 'What's an *Edict* when it's at home?' We all look at him. Here was a staunch man, in the face of certain ridicule, prepared to show his ignorance in the hope of enlightenment. And if he's not taking the piss that is, we'll give him the benefit of the doubt and trust that his secondary school education had not got as far as covering such complex vocabulary.

The Father gives him a stare of disbelief. A man, seeing it as his duty to inscribe a degree of good grammar into proceedings is now being thwarted.

'I cannot believe that men who work with the Queen's English on a daily basis are not familiar with words like *Edict*.'

He is not only an unbeliever, neither is he going to demean himself by explaining the definition.

'I suggest that those of you that don't know the meaning of the word consult *Oxford English* for the refurbishment of their Mother tongue, I will continue with the rest that do. The *Edict* . . . that has come down from head office . . .'

He was absolutely right, of course; but you just don't go around saying such things to your fellow workers that elected you and to whom you are supposed to represent. You are all, after all, on a level playing field. And even if you weren't there is nothing more demeaning to another than to highlight the deficiencies of another's education by suggesting he go look up definitions in a dictionary.

The Chapel was beginning to look angry.

What he should have done; and what I would have done after it had become apparent that a word was not understood by all was to have changed it to another that everyone, including the lowest denominator, who through no fault of his own had not had the benefit of one's own higher education – Comprehensive, in my own case. I would have begun:

'The *Ukase* . . . that has come down from head office . . .' *Then*, we would have all known what the hell he was on about; and he would not have been forced to resign after being politely asked to stand down.

All Chapel meetings attended by us in the ad-setting and repro business were of the nature mild in comparison to what was going on in the London newspapers. Here strict lines of demarcation were adhered to with a ruthlessness to the point of idiocy. Spanish Practices were invented in Fleet Street. You had to be careful what you touched if it was out of the sphere of your trade even if the line was blurred. A Press Manager would not be allowed to recover bundles of papers from the stack coming off the Press. He would be NGA (Machine Branch); that would be a job for NATSOPA. He would be allowed to recover sufficient copies to check for quality and that was all. A Pressman would not be allowed to remove battered type from a forme; but he would be allowed to push down spaces that had risen. It could be a minefield. I am reminded of ship builders' that had to drill in the hull of a ship. The shipwright could only drill as far into the steel to a wooden lining; here it was the job of the carpenter to continue.

The introduction of new technologies outside of newspapers and in the provinces, like lithography, where compositors (NGA), for instance, working with new phototypesetting machines had to have bromides developed by camera operators (SLADE). By the time, an agreement had been reached between the separate unions for some common sense another piece of technology came along, making the other obsolete before it could be written into the rule book. Generally speaking, issues could be resolved while you had operators of different unions working under one roof, where it became difficult was outside work coming in from sources unknown. Advertisements were coming into provincial newspapers and magazines being presented as camera-ready copy. A bromide that had been cut and pasted by what should have been compositors but was often produced by people that were totally unqualified were creeping into the industry. Not that anyone needed to be particularly qualified to cut and paste but that was not the point the NGA decided that a line was to be drawn in the sand. A line that they had not a cat in hell's chance of maintaining. Nevertheless, it was decided that all camera ready copy would have to carry an NGA sticker with the source name of the company printed on it. It worked to a certain extent in that at least you knew, even if you didn't like the new technology, that it had come from people that were time-served compositor craftsmen. But it was only a matter of time before even that by sheer volume fell apart and the thin end of the proverbial wedge drove into the root of the NGA. Faced with such challenges the NGA amalgamated with SOGAT in 1990 becoming the Graphical, Paper & Media, before merging with Amicus in 2004 which in turn amalgamated with the T&GWU becoming known as UNITE in 2007; all a dilution into obscurity. The ss *Spinning Jenny* had arrived back in dock, as it had so often in the past, and it was no longer a vessel that could be turned back.

23 – THE END OF THE LINE

A COMPOSITOR is not a printer. Although he did work in the printing industry. And it is for that reason – although printing has continued very much as it always has – that I momentarily turned my back on the industry. For when the art of composing went the way of the dinosaur, I followed it.

When as a young boy, I had been given a John Bull Printing outfit for Christmas, as so many other boys of my age had, it became an inspiration. Small rubber letters that could be set into a wooden block and printed, with the aid of an ink block onto paper, was like today's younger generation seeing Mine Craft for the first time. The likes of Mine Craft and other games capable of being played out on mobile phones and tablets will undoubtedly lead this new generation and its following into a world of electronics, coding, familiarity with HTML, Twitter, Instagram and the rest. The John Bull Printing outfit was my Mine Craft of the day and as I got older you would find me after school standing in the front door of the Tooting and Balham Gazette offices watching the compositors taking type from the cases and using them for the weekly newspaper. I had always had a high regard for the setting of lead type into lines of justified length one upon the other until eventually becoming a page. I have never regarded printing in the same way.

Printing to me – and with no disrespect to my brother Keith – was a mundane process upon which, by its nature and its invention, once the finished composed origination had been set into the Press's platen, the quality of each impression was constant, the ink was in the ducts, then the printers job was done, the Press would churn out copy after copy *ad infinitum*. There may well be more to it than my perceived view of the process and what I know, I'm sure there is, but I choose to dismiss it. It pales against the fleeting kiss of crude paper passing over the composed face of descenders, ascenders and kerns that knew its days were numbered.

Although I did accommodate the new technology, I had lost control of hard metal that had ghosted itself, lost forever in computers. Many said it was an interesting time this modernisation of the production of the composed word that had now become devoid of life. It might well have been. I can say that I grasped it, learnt the new methods, became an origination manager for a major company producing national four-colour magazines and the like. It had turned into a nuts and bolts industry where every full-point had to be accounted for along with scanned pics; but I had eventually fast lost interest in even that. The confirmation of working with people that I was constantly trying to teach even the most basic of typographical procedures became all too much in the end. Watching them re-invent the wheel was like pulling teeth; dismissing them in their achievements, not out of any sense of rudeness more of watching all that I had learned being dumped into the dustbin of history without any heed from those that if they'd had bothered to ask, just might have known the truth, saving an awful lot of time.

24 – PRINTING TRADE TERMS

A Chapel – A meeting of compositors is called a Chapel, and the members of the Chapel form a companionship (shortened to 'ship) pledged to watch over the interests of the union and its members in the Chapel.

A Wrong Fount – A wrong fount is a letter of a different fount found among the correct fount. A shady kind of fellow is also referred to as a 'wrong fount'.

An Out – When a compositor accidentally omits a word or a phrase it is termed an 'out', and if several words are missing the reader writes in the margin of the proof: Out See Copy and pins the copy to the proof for return to the compositor for correction.

Bridging – A compositor is said to have 'bridged' if he fails to appear at the appointed time to put the line on and forwards no reason for his absence.

Chopper On – A companion is choppery when he is surly and unapproachable and therefore looks hatchet-faced hence: having a chopper on.

Clerk of the Chapel – A member elected to act as secretary at meetings, take and read minutes, collect subscriptions and dues, prepare Chapel sheets, pay Chapel money into the Society, and give each quarter a proper account of Chapel events. The Father and the Clerk are the only responsible officials recognised by the Union on the Chapel's behalf.

Cocking a Deaf 'Un – Pretending not to hear something particularly addressed to oneself.

Cutting the Line – When a mealtime break is due, the Father of the Chapel calls, 'Cut the line, gentlemen', and each compositor stops work, resuming when the Father calls 'Line on, gentlemen'. All piece hands must have an equal chance of the work provided, and in this manner it is ensured. The copy provided by the Printer is lifted according to the Chapel rota. When the last page is sent into the foundry the Father 'cuts the line' and announces the number of men required to stop for the next edition; the others go home.

Earwigging – Listening to conversation that is intended to be private.

Fat – Work easy of performance at adequate rates.

Father of the Chapel – A compositor elected by his fellows to see that the customs of the trade, scales, condition of work, etc. are strictly followed, and disputes avoided. No other member of the Chapel is allowed to interview the Printer or Management unless accompanied by the Father.

Front Pages, Back Pages, and Side Pages – Where two compositors are working side by side they are known as side pages; where three are working, the one in the middle refers to his companions as 'my right-hand side page' and 'my left-hand side page'; if men are working back to back they are known as back pages; if frames or machines are set facing each other, the men are front pages.

G.H. – Is an expression which means that the one who uses it is indicating to another that the one treating of a subject under discussion should go home and teach his grandmother to suck eggs. When a piece of stale news is related the cry goes around, 'G.H.!' Meaning of initials is lost in time.

Gobblers – A gobbler is a fast-setting compositor who 'gobbles' as much copy as he can set. In the general trade a gobbler is one who does as much overtime as possible.

K.D. – The meaning is to keep anything dark; that is, not relate it outside the present company. Particularly used when private work was being undertaken surreptitiously.

Knowing Your Boxes – Being aware of what you are doing or talking about. One of the first things an apprentice compositor is taught is the layout of the upper and lower cases, which means the geography of the types contained in them.

Machine Compositor – Is a compositor with the added knowledge of the Linotype, Intertype, Monotype, Ludlow, etc. He is usually called an operator or op.

Miles's Boy – Miles was a printer in the old days, whose apprentice was knowing and artful: to whom all sorts of news came. Hence: 'according to Miles's Boy'.

Nailing – To nail is to talk derogatively (usually in a quiet fashion) of another compositor.

The Nailbox – A mythical box full of nails, long and short, which are said to be driven into a person who is absent.

N.F. – A fish rises to a fly as bait: a companion who hears or observes something intended for him and ignores it is said to be 'no fly'.

'No, You Don't!' – This means that information given, or relation

of action taken, is not believed by the others present; and heads are shaken as the words go forth: 'No, You Don't!'

On the Coach – In stage-coach travelling times, if one person wished to avoid another during the journey he would seek an inside seat while the other had perforce to travel outside high up on the coach. If two compositors fall out (publicly or privately) they would avoid each other. Companions are quick to notice this in the Chapel, and the word goes around: 'Bill's got Jasper on the coach'.

On the Stone – Taking a compositor away from one class of work and putting him at work on a page waiting to be sent to press. The stone is an imposing surface on which pages are prepared for press. It is of metal but was formerly a flat stone.

Pica-thumpers – For the benefit of laymen, Pica refers to a size of type used in the old days largely for Parliamentary and similar work. Thumping was the lifting of the types from the cases into the composing sticks. Hence, 'pica-thumpers', a term applying, in fact, to all hand piece-workers. The coming of the composing machine displaced them.

Piece Work – Work paid for at the rates laid down in the piece scales.

Pieing Your Case – To pie a case is accidentally to mix the letters so that they have to be sorted out and put in the right boxes.

Putting the Line On – When compositors are engaged on piece work each must be ready to start to set his first line when the Father calls 'Line On'. Copy is lifted simultaneously, and work begins. This is known as the 'simultaneous lift' and was strictly observed in daily paper companionships.

Putting up the Half-Double – A half-double rule was always printed at the end of an article. Therefore, 'to put up the half-double' is to end conversation on a particular subject between compositors.

Ratting – Working under the recognised rates.

Spiking – When copy is left incomplete, or taken away before the article is finished, it is 'spiked' with a bradawl, and if it is returned later the compositor to whom it is given to resume setting calls it 'taking up the spike'. (The author still uses this mode of marking of a place in text with the word: Spike.)

Stab Work – Work paid for at the established weekly rate.

Takes – A 'take' is a piece of copy set by the compositor.

The House – This means the Society (Union) house; the London Society of Compositors.

The Organ – A mutual club formed by compositors and paid for by them at so much per week, enabling those who wish, to borrow money and repay with interest to the secretary, or Organ Master, as he was known.

The Printer, and the 'O' – An 'O' or overseer of a paper—that is, he who is in charge and is responsible for seeing the pages off the stone to the foundry or the machine room—is also known as 'the Bloke'. So is an overseer of a composing room. He who is responsible for the paper is called a Printer, while the 'O' or overseer may be responsible for a great variety of jobs, is never called the Printer.

The Slate is Up – A slate is provided in each office where piece workers are employed. When a compositor finishes his 'take' and finds no more copy to lift, he writes his name on the slate and waits for work, calling out, 'Slate Up'. When there is more copy, 'takes' are lifted in the order of names on the slate.

The Swinger – The last 'take' of copy in the box is termed 'the swinger', and to 'grab the swinger' is to drop the 'take' just set and get to the copy box before other striving companions, who have disconsolately to put up the slate.

Trots and Trotting – Leading a companions 'up the garden path'.

Whack! – When compositors are gathered together and a tall story is told, or it be doubted that the truth has been told by a speaker, a whack with the composing stick on the frame is given as an indication of un-philosophic doubt.

Wrong Cast-Off – To estimate something incorrectly. A compositor will say to another who has made a wrong statement through guesswork: 'You've made a wrong cast-off'.

You Can! – This is a phrase that increases or decreases in effect by inflection as it is pronounced. It means that the speaker presents to his hearers the whole matter under discussion for them to do with as they wish. There was once a compositor who was called, 'You Can Have It Jones', on account of his deprecatory attitude to the whole universe.

That's it, Gents! and Lasses!
Cool, Fine, Done, Wicked!

BIBLIOGRAPHY/ ACKNOWLEDGEMENTS

The
MAUREEN & KEITH JACKSON
Family

THE 'LINE' IS ON,
George E. Rowles,
LONDON SOCIETY OF COMPOSITORS (1948)

THE LONDON SOCIETY OF COMPOSITORS,
A CENTENARY HISTORY,
Ellic Howe and Harold E. Waite,
CASSELL & COMPANY (1948)

FRONT COVER HALF-TONE:
Case and Stick courtesy of
WIKIPEDIA, PUBLIC DOMAIN

150 FASCINATING TUBE FACTS
The Telegraph Online

COOL, FINE, DONE, WICKED!
With acknowledgements to the sentiments of
Craig David from his *Born To Do It* album

BIOGRAPHY

Mr. Jackson was born in Wandsworth, south London. He left school at sixteen to begin a career in the old Covent Garden district of London. As an apprentice compositor he composed in London's burgeoning advertising industry.

Attending what is now the London College of Communication he studied hand composition, graphic art and typography. The typography gave him an interest in ancient writing and the City College at Aldersgate and Barbican – along the old London Wall – taught him that cuneiform was not a way forward in his career.

With his love of the sea – sub-aqua diving in particular – he moved to Plymouth with his then girlfriend, Rita. At a local branch of the British Sub-Aqua Club, he became their training officer.

In his professional life he worked as an origination manager for several print companies. From there he set up his own typesetting business originating books and magazines. He now runs a graphics and print business using his know-how to produce e-Books and ePaperbacks.

With her permission, he married his girlfriend, Rita. A Surrey rose – they have three children and two grandchildren.

A WORD FROM THE AUTHOR

Most indie authors don't benefit from the massive promotions afforded by publishing houses or book shops, their only promotional ability is by social media or word of mouth, and while those limitations may suit the conventional book trade (agents and publishers), for indie authors it's their only book shop window. The fact that you use the facilities of independent publishing outlets, tells me that you are in favour of seeking out books that would otherwise not see the light of day. For myself, I do not pay for reviews; neither am I on social media, trusting instead to my readers for any accolades or criticisms they may have to review on the source of purchase.

Good Luck, and Peace to you All,

Gil Jackson

OTHER BOOKS BY THE AUTHOR

Available on most Indie Publishing platforms

www.ingramcontent.com/pod-product-compliance
Lightning Source LLC
Chambersburg PA
CBHW021436080526
44588CB00009B/549